...Immigration Wars

The History of U.S. American Immigration Policies

by Ira Zornberg

This book is dedicated to people who demonstrated the courage to immigrate and begin life anew. This book is also dedicated to those who report accurately on issues related to immigration at the present time and seek to provide understanding to those who are empowered to make future immigration laws.

A special thanks to my wife, Judith Zornberg, for editing and formatting this book.

Table of Contents

Chapter 1 –Immigration: An Emotional Subject

If we accept the premise that people whom European explorers found in the Americas (Native Americans) were themselves part of a migration of peoples, immigrants who preceded Europeans to the Americas, it would make the unfinished story of immigrants coming to this country easier to tell. It may well be the best framework because it is the most inclusive.

Accepting that thesis does not mitigate the fact that European immigrants were unkind to those who preceded them, nor that twenty percent of all Americans, after the American Revolution, were involuntary immigrants, enslaved and brought from Africa as a source of labor. This last point is very important because it accurately and rightly includes Africans among immigrants to this land.

It is not an exaggeration to say that the U.S. has been the most welcoming nation to immigrants of any nation on earth. Even people from nations once excluded from immigration and naturalization continue to seek homes in the United States. An accurate account of our history must also describe exclusionary policies directed against people deemed undesirable because of race and religion, policies that closed our doors to refugees who would otherwise perish.

Americans today are bitterly divided over what U.S. immigration policies should be. "Build the wall" has become the symbolic cry of people who believe in the need to limit immigration, especially of illegal or undocumented immigrants. Most Americans agree on the need to secure our border, but are uncertain as to how to address it. Most favor providing a path to citizenship for young people, brought to the U.S. as children by undocumented parents, but Congress has failed to provide it.

Indicative of how divisive the politics of immigration has become, many cities have declared themselves "sanctuary cities" in which government officials have been forbidden to share identities and locations of undocumented aliens with ICE (Immigration and Customs Enforcement Agency empowered to deport illegal aliens). The most radical voices call for the abolition of ICE. Such conflict between federal and local authorities has not been experienced since federal troops were required to desegregate public schools in the south in the 1950s and 1960s. No moral equivalence is implied between present day issues over immigration and ending racial segregation. What is disturbing is the defiance of federal law and the disquieting and divisive nature of the struggle.

Between 1965 and 2015, 45 million immigrants legally entered the U.S. and now constitute 14% of the U.S. population. Technological change, "outsourcing" and a decline in American manufacturing jobs left many Americans economically insecure. Many were angered by news stories of illegal immigrants working for low wages in meat packing plants. With one million immigrants legally entering the U.S. each year, their anger is focused on the more than 11 million undocumented aliens presently in the U.S.

A recent development has been robust economic growth during the past year and in some sectors an actual shortage of labor. In the article *Immigration Debate Misses EconomicReality,* Gerald R. Seib wrote:

> There is a good case that America's economy – growing and thriving- has never needed immigrant labor more than it does now....more than a third of businesses have job openings they can't fill... The fertility rate for women aged 15-44 was 60,2 per thousand women, the lowest since the government began tracking... in the next

three decades, the share of Americans aged 65 and older will surpass the share of Americans 18 and younger.... Put it all together and you have a picture of a country that not only can handle immigrants, but one that should want them and actually may need them. Yet, the climate is more hostile toward immigrants and immigration than at any time in recent memory. (*Wall Street Journal*, May 22, 2018)

On June 6, 2018, in an editorial, *Now Hiring Everywhere* the *Wall Street Journal* stated, "If President Trump really wants business to stay in America, he's going to have to reconsider his hostility to immigration." Statistical charts below indicate jobs held by undocumented immigrants. (*Wall Street Journal Editorial Board*, June 6, 2018)

IV. Top 20 Jobs Held (2008) by Immigrants Living in the United States Illegally

Top 20 Jobs Held, 2008

Top 20 Occupations*	# of Immigrant Workers in the US Illegally	Total # of All Workers	% of Immigrants in the US Illegally in Total Work Force
1. Brickmasons, blockmasons, and stonemasons	131,000	325,000	40%
2. Drywall installers,	94,000	255,000	37%

ceiling tile installers and tapers			
3. Roofers	76,000	246,000	31%
4. Miscellaneous agricultural workers	269,000	910,000	30%
5. Helpers, construction trades	52,000	184,000	28%
6. Dishwashers	101,000	364,000	28%
7. Construction laborers	556,000	2,055,000	27%
8. Maids and housekeepers	417,000	1,555,000	27%
9. Cement Masons, concrete finishers, and terrazzo workers	29,000	109,000	27%
10. Packaging and filling machine operators and tenders	96,000	369,000	26%
11. Grounds maintenance workers	356,000	1,413,000	25%
12. Packers and packagers, hand	119,000	504,000	24%
13. Butchers, poultry and fish processing workers	71,000	305,000	23%
14. Carpet, floor, and tile installers and finishers	68,000	306,000	22%
15. Painters, construction and maintenance	173,000	791,000	22%
16. Parking lot attendants	21,000	100,000	21%
17. Chefs and head cooks	75,000	377,000	20%
18. Sewing machine operators	49,000	248,000	20%
19. Refuse and recyclable material	22,000	112,000	19%

collectors			
20. Cooks	427,000	2,219,000	19%
Other "unauthorized" occupations**	3,120,000	34,979,000	9%
All other occupations	1,928,000	106,407,000	2%
Total, Civilian Labor Force (with an occupation)	8,258,000	154,135,000	5%

(https://immigration.procon.org/view.resource.php?resourceID=000845)

It remains to be seen if improved economic conditions change the thinking of fearful Americans.

Since September 11, 2001, when thousands of Americans were murdered by Islamic terrorists who legally entered the U.S., national security has become a pivotal concern in shaping the immigration debate. Many have questioned the wisdom of policies that allowed terrorists to obtain and overstay their visas. It was an Egyptian immigrant, granted a visa through the Immigrant Diversity Program, who took flying lessons in the U.S. and piloted an airliner filled with commuters into a tower of New York's World Trade Center. The presidential debates of 2016 witnessed a clash of positions. For humanitarian reasons, Hillary Clinton supported the admission of additional numbers of Syrian refugees, while Donald Trump advocated their exclusion.

In the article, *Immigration Debate...* cited above, Seib recognized another important element fostering debate over immigration. He wrote "...the anti-immigrant mood is rooted in...an understandable feeling among many Americans that they are losing control of their country and its traditions..." (*Wall Street Journal*, June 6, 2018) Implied, if not openly stated, is that many American citizens who are white, Christian and of European extraction increasingly feel ill at ease with what they see as the rapidly changing demographic makeup in the United States. If the projection issued by the Bureau of the Census for 2050 is correct, the population of the United States will look dramatically different in 2050 from what it is today.

Following are two graphs which project demographic change. Whereas the first one projects that the immigrant percentage of the population will be greatest in U.S. history, the second one predicts that only 52.8% of the population will be non-Hispanic white (mostly of European extraction) by 2050. There are people who find this upsetting.

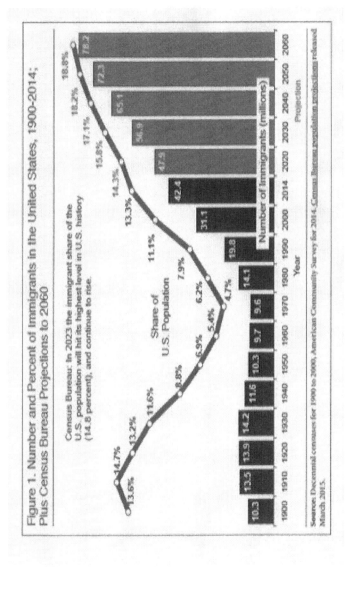

Figure 1. Number and Percent of Immigrants in the United States, 1900-2014; Plus Census Bureau Projections to 2060

Census Bureau: In 2023 the immigrant share of the U.S. population will hit its highest level in U.S. history (14.8 percent), and continue to rise.

Share of U.S. Population

Number of Immigrants (millions)

Source: Decennial censuses for 1900 to 2000, American Community Survey for 2014. Census Bureau population projections released March 2015.

8

Projected Changes in the Ethnic and Racial Composition of the United States, 2000-2050
(Percentage of total U.S. population)

Year	White, non-Hispanic	Black, non-Hispanic	Asian & Pacific Islander	Hispanic
2000	71.8	12.2	3.9	11.4
2005	69.9	12.4	4.4	12.6
2010	68.0	12.6	4.8	13.8
2015	66.1	12.7	5.3	15.1
2020	64.3	12.9	5.7	16.3
2025	62.4	13.0	6.2	17.6
2030	60.5	13.1	6.6	18.9
2035	58.6	13.2	7.1	20.3
2040	56.7	13.3	7.5	21.7
2045	54.7	13.5	7.9	23.1
2050	52.8	13.6	8.2	24.5

Source: U.S. Bureau of the Census, Current Population Reports, Series P25-1130, "Population Projections of the United States by Age, Sex, Race, and Hispanic Origin, 1995 to 2050." March, 1997. Washington, D.C.: U.S. Government Printing Office.

Both the right and left fringes of the American political spectrum interpret statistics in disquieting ways. Radicals on the left speak of new immigrants as "people of color," and potential allies in their struggle against the "white racist establishment." Far right white extremists, some wearing Nazi symbols, portray themselves as defenders of the white race. In their alternative realities, both refuse to consider the reasons immigrants come to America. Both raise disquieting voices and stir emotions.

Fueling the disquieting debate is the large scale migration from Central America. Driven by violence and economic hardship, migrants continue to move across U.S. borders. There are two ways undocumented persons (lacking visas obtained from U.S. consulates in their native countries) can enter the U.S. The first is to go to a U.S. immigration border post at a point of entry and ask for asylum. Here they may be held up for days or weeks. When admitted, they explain their "credible fears" of losing their lives to violence in their home countries and ask for asylum. They are aware that such claims will allow their admission, at least until a hearing by an immigration judge. It is known that the backlog for such hearings will take years to eliminate.

The second way to get into the U.S. (without a visa) is run or walk across its borders. In March, April and May 2018, tens of thousands crossed the Mexican border into the U.S. Most came from Honduras, Guatemala and El Salvador. To deter this flow, Attorney General Sessions announced a "zero tolerance policy," requiring the arrest, trial and sentencing of those who enter illegally. Since the Flores Agreement, a part of U.S. case law, forbids the housing of children in prison facilities, even with their parents, a policy of separating children from their parents was adopted. Visuals of crying children being separated from parents produced an outcry so great that President Trump responded with an executive order ending the practice.

There is now a need for Congress to act. Securing the borders of the United States and deciding the fate of undocumented or illegal immigrants already within our country are imperatives. Deciding the numbers and skills of those to be legally admitted must be part of a comprehensive updated immigration policy. Understanding past policies and their effects, positive and negative, is essential in designing policies for the future. It is the purpose of this book to contribute to such understanding.

Chapter 2 – Our First Census

Immigration to the United States began before Americans won their independence from England. It began with European exploration and colonization in the 16th century, followed by the involuntary immigration of Africans. The nature of this earliest immigration was decided before the American Revolution. It was determined by the welcoming or exclusionary policies in each of the colonies. In the Biblical *Book of Numbers,* we are told that only two months after the exodus from Egypt, Moses ordered tribal leaders to conduct a census among his people. He wanted to evaluate his human assets. The Constitution of the United States, ratified in 1789 mandated that a census be taken every ten years and our first national government under the constitution ordered the first census in 1790. It is through this first census that we learn who had immigrated prior to that time. The census was taken by federal marshals in each district who would go from one residence to another and conduct a count.

The Constitution states that both representation and taxation will be apportioned after a count of the American people. The count would include all free persons and three-fifths of all others. Who were the others? They were Africans or people descended from Africans, involuntary immigrants. In order to convince southern delegates (from states with relatively small populations of free persons) to ratify the Constitution, they were allowed to count 3/5 of their slaves in determining their population and representation in Congress. It was both the need to determine congressional representation and the requirement for a census every ten years that led to the census in 1790. It would take three years before data would be made known. It produced the first account of who lived within the borders of the United States.

The Constitution granted Congress the power to establish a "uniform rule of naturalization." It would establish the conditions and the process by which an alien could apply for and be naturalized (granted citizenship).

Bureaucrats formulated the questions to be asked by census takers. Information was to be listed in the following categories; "free white males over 16," "free white males under 16," "free white females," "slaves," and "all other free persons." The last category related to free black people or free people of mixed race. Race consciousness is evident. Data collected would "be

submitted to the president." Conclusions are indicated
in the chart below.

District	Free white males of 16 years and upward, including heads of families.	Free white males under 16 years.	Free white females, including heads of families.	All other free persons.	Slaves.	Total.
Vermont	22,435	22,328	40,505	255	16[a][6]	85,539[b]
New Hampshire	36,086	34,851	70,160	630	158	141,885
Maine	24,384	24,748	46,870	538	0	96,540
Massachusetts	95,453	87,289	190,582	5,463	0	378,787[c][7]
Rhode Island	16,019	15,799	32,652	3,407	948	68,825
Connecticut	60,523	54,403	117,448	2,808	2,764	237,946
New York	83,700	78,122	152,320	4,654	21,324	340,120
New Jersey	45,251	41,416	83,287	2,762	11,423	184,139
Pennsylvania	110,788	106,948	206,363	6,537	3,737	434,373
Delaware	11,783	12,143	22,384	3,899	8,887	59,094[d]
Maryland	55,915	51,339	101,395	8,043	103,036	319,728
Virginia	110,936	116,135	215,046	12,866	292,627	747,610[e][7]
Kentucky	15,154	17,057	28,922	114	12,430	73,677
North Carolina	69,988	77,506	140,710	4,975	100,572	393,751
South Carolina	35,576	37,722	66,880	1,801	107,094	249,073
Georgia	13,103	14,044	25,739	398	29,264	82,548
Total	807,094	791,850	1,541,263	59,150	694,280	3,893,635

Below is a chart estimating the numbers of people in each ethnic group which immigrated and their numbers in 1790 due to natural increase. Of the 3.9 million inhabitants living within the territorial borders of the U.S., 2,560,000 (80% of the population) were of British origin. Included were immigrants from England, Scotland, Ireland (mostly Scotch-Irish) and Wales. The original 360,000 from England had multiplied to 2,100,000. The second largest source of immigration was African. An estimated 360,000 African arrivals had multiplied to an estimated 757,000 by 1790.

U.S. Historical Populations		
Country	Immigrants Before 1790	Population 1790 -1
Africa -2	360,000	757,000
England*	230,000	2,100,000
Ulster Scot-Irish*	135,000	300,000
Germany -3	103,000	270,000
Scotland*	48,500	150,000
Ireland*	8,000	(Incl. in Scot-Irish)
Netherlands	6,000	100,000
Wales*	4,000	10,000
France	3,000	15,000
Jews -4	1,000	2,000
Sweden	500	2,000
Other -5	50,000	200,000
Total -6	950,000	3,900,000

(https://en.wikipedia.org/wiki/Demographic_history_of_the_U nited_States#Population_in_1790)

Last names were used to identify Europeans. The census indicated that there were 270,000 from Germany, 15,000 from France (primarily Huguenots-Protestants by religion), 2,000 from Sweden and 2,000 Jews (mostly of Sephardic origin, who traced their ancestry to Spain). The census identified Jews as a separate nationality.

An explanation of how New England's thirteen colonies were populated requires an understanding of both England's colonial policies and the attitudes and laws governing immigration, which existed in each colony.

Chapter 3 - British Policy and Colonial Laws

To benefit from the resources and develop the land of their claims in North America, England gave charters to companies and individuals who promised to populate their colonies. Fearful of reducing its own population, England permitted colonization companies to transport foreigners, mostly Protestants displaced by religious wars in their home countries. To encourage immigration, colonial governors signed letters of "denization" which granted citizenship and equality with English settlers. To serve its own economic interests there were times when colonial laws limiting immigration were disallowed by England's General Court. In 1641, in its Body of Liberties, Massachusetts Bay, using Biblical language stated that there shall be no bond slavery; it was nullified in England as was Maryland's law prohibiting the importation of convicts. In the book, *Colonial Immigration Laws*, Edron E. Proper, wrote, "…it is to the English government and to the proprietors of the provinces that the larger share of credit must be given for fostering immigration."

(https://thefederalistpapers.org/wp-Immigration-laws.pdf)

Only in the 1770's, when the possibility of revolution became a reality, was the presence of great numbers of immigrants from countries other than Britain blamed for radicalism. In 1773, colonial governors were directed to stop naturalization. The preamble to a law in 1774 declared, "the great increase of the people has in the said colonies had an immediate tendency to produce independency." (*Colonial Immigration Laws, p. 201.* Among the charges leveled at the king in the Declaration of Independence was that "He has endeavored to prevent the population of these states, for that purpose obstructing Laws for Naturalization of Foreigners, refusing to pass others to encourage their migrations hither…"

While the policies of the mother country provided the framework for colonial immigration and settlement, the policies and laws of each colony were important in determining the number who settled, their ethnicity and religion.

Virginia

As incentives for immigration by freemen, Virginia offered land for each settler, exemptions from taxation, and in 1669 passed a law forbidding the collection of debts contracted before immigrating. Between 1650 and

1776 an estimated 20,000 people who would be indentured servants arrived. About 4,000 were women. Most came as "redemptioners," people for whom ship captains paid the passage. If relatives claimed an arrival they would pay his fee. If not, an immigrant would be auctioned off and sold into indentured servitude. In a period which could last as many as seven years, indentured servants promised not to marry without the permission of one's master, promised to work and not run away. All the possessions and the labor of the servant belonged to the owner. Servants could be traded and families could be divided. Additional time could be added to the service of a woman who became pregnant, even if the one who fathered her child was her master. Courts enforced the contracts. At one point, three fourths of all immigrants were indentured servants.

In return for provisions, a Dutch ship deposited the first Africans in Virginia in 1619. Initially they were given indentures (contracts for fixed periods of labor) but over the next forty years law makers extended their terms of service for life and then to the status of property in slave codes. The case of John Punch notes the evolution of Africans from indentured servants to slavery. Paunch ran away and violated his indenture. While two white men who did so had their terms increased, the governor of Virginia in 1640 sentenced Pauch to a life in servitude. (https://en/wikipedia.org/wiki/John_Paunch_slave)

Among European immigrants were small numbers of Polish, Slovene and French Protestants, refugees from Catholic regions in Europe. Scotch-Irish Immigrants settled along Virginia's western frontier. Thomas Jefferson was descended from Welsh immigrants. Virginia became a royal colony in 1624

In the census of 1790, Virginia with its population of 747,559 was the most populous state. 292,627 (39%) were slaves (mostly from the Niger Delta). Africans brought to America involuntarily were counted in our first national census. The census also noted that 12,366 non-white free people lived in Virginia in 1790 (many were of mixed race).

Virginia did not count members of Native American tribes as Virginians. It is estimated that 100,000 Native Americans belonging to different tribes lived within the borders of the United States in 1790. After independence, the United States followed Virginia's model. It negotiated with each tribe as if it was a separate nation. Not until 1924 and an act of Congress were Native Americans recognized as citizens of the United States.

Massachusetts

The Anglican Church or Church of England was established by King Henry VIII in 1533. There were many dissenters who refused to follow its directives. Pilgrims, Christians who believed in congregational practice, first migrated to Holland and then established Plymouth Plantation in 1620. Puritans, who had hoped to reform that church but failed, determined to build a faith based society of their own in the new world. Supposedly seeking a charter for an economic enterprise like that of the Virginia stock holders, they obtained a charter and a land grant for approximately fifteen square miles in 1628. With charter in hand (so it would be difficult to revoke), Puritans began a mass migration to America. John Winthrop led a fleet of eleven ships with 800 people to New England and 20,000 followed in the next ten years.

The Puritans viewed themselves as a religious community with a divine mission, their aim to establish "a new Jerusalem," "a City on a Hill." John Winthrop, who was to repeatedly serve as governor of the Massachusetts Bay Colony, wrote, "...we here be a

corporation established by free consent…no man hath a right to come into without our consent."
(https://thefederalistpapers.org/ebooks/colonial-immigration-laws)

The Puritans established a theocracy. Salaries of the ministers were provided by the colony, whose approval was required before one could be granted freeman status (the ability to vote). Lawmakers were elected by the freemen. Religious faith could be uplifting as was the creation of Harvard College in 1634, or it could be a source of anguish as was witnessed in the Salem Witchcraft trials and executions in 1692.

Intent on preserving their society, as a measure of security, many restrictions were imposed on persons who could enter and live in the colony. The admission of foreigners required the approval of ministers. A fine of up to 100 pounds could be levied on any person bringing in strangers without permission. Noting their progress in converting Native Americans to Catholicism, Jesuits were denied entry to the colony in 1647.

Guided by Biblical injunction against slavery, a law in 1647 required that Africans be returned to their own country. It was disallowed in Britain. In 1705, vessels were required to pay a 4 pound tax on each Negro imported. The law was never reported to England. It is interesting that despite the many New England merchants involved in the slave trade that the census of 1790 did not indicate the presence of a single slave in that colony.

In 1700, the Plymouth colony was joined with the Massachusetts Bay Colony. In 1730, a community of Huguenots (French Protestants) was legalized. A restrictive law in 1756 denied admission to "sick, impotent or infirm persons."

Among the few Jews who arrived from Holland, one was compelled to return to Holland, while a second became the resident Hebrew teacher at Harvard after converting to Christianity. The first Jewish family is believed to have settled in New Haven Connecticut in 1772.

The most punitive exclusionary policy was directed against Quakers. Founded by George Fox in the early 17th century, members of the Society of Friends were commonly called Quakers. Like the Puritans, they refused to adhere to the dictates of the Anglican Church, but they also challenged the theocratic organization of Massachusetts Bay. They refused to take oaths of loyalty to church or state. The Quakers preached that common people could communicate with God through an "inner light" and do God's will. Quakers rejected clergy and tithes, were pacifists, refusing to serve in the military (where they would be compelled to take a human life), were opposed to slavery, and initially allowed women to preach and play a greater role in the church. Believing that they were following the model of Christ they felt compelled to preach. Their books were burned and their missionaries were jailed and expelled in 1657. Upon returning in 1659, two men and a woman (Mary Dyes) were put to death.

The Census of 1790 indicates that the population of Massachusetts was 378,787, second to that of Virginia, with 0 as the number of slaves.

Connecticut

Connecticut was founded by the learned Puritan preacher Thomas Hooker in 1636. His petition to leave for Connecticut was granted by the General Court of Massachusetts. One deviation from Massachusetts law was that one could become a freeman and vote without the approval of a church. Its reported population in 1790 was 237,946 which included 2,764 slaves and 2,808 non-white persons who were free.

Rhode Island

Colonial leaders of Massachusetts Bay had little patience for dissenters in their own midst. Roger Williams, a Puritan minister in Salem became an advocate of separating church and state so that the church could remain pure, free from the corrupting influence of politics. He advocated more humane treatment of Native Americans. He was banished from the colony in mid-winter, fled southward and was assisted by the Narragansett Tribe in establishing a new colony which he called Providence (meaning God will provide). Roger Williams established the first Baptist Church in America and his *Key to the Language of America* made native language intelligible. Rhode Island received a charter for self-government from Charles II in 1663. Settlement was open to people of all religious faiths. Quakers, Catholics and Jews settled in Rhode Island. The first synagogue in America was built in Newport. Wars in the 1670's following his death virtually destroyed the Narragansets. The growth of the colony was slow; its numbers increased after Newport became a hub of the slave trade. Its total population in 1790 was 68,825. There were 948 slaves and 3,047 were free persons of color.

New York

The Dutch model for settlement in new lands was to establish trading posts rather than populate those areas. Dutch merchants had briefly traded for furs with native tribes in the early 1600's. In 1621, the States General chartered the Dutch West India Company and gave it a monopoly over trade with Africa and America between the 40th and 45th parallels. Its claim was based upon the exploration of Henry Hudson in 1609. The Dutch West India Company established trading posts in Albany and New Amsterdam (on the island of Manhattan), called their colony the New Netherlands, and entertained the idea of populating their new colony.

To encourage settlement, land grants were given to patroons (resembling medieval lords) for each colonist brought to the New Netherlands. Failing to attract many settlers, permission was given to permit any settler to buy land. Population figures are imprecise, but it is believed that New Amsterdam's population was 270 in 1628, 500 in 1640 and 10,000 in 1660.

The best remembered governor of New Amsterdam was Peter Stuyvesant. By 1664, the New Netherlands had extended its control over the Jerseys and over New Sweden (established in 1638 in what became Delaware). A wall was built mostly by enslaved Africans to secure

New Amsterdam against a possible Lenape (the Native American tribe most prevalent in the area) attack. Stuyvesant had hoped to make New Amsterdam a center of the slave trade.

Five hundred Africans, believed to have come mostly from the Angola region lived in the colony by 1660. By paying a tax and being subject to recall for labor, Africans could live in their own homes, a status known as "half freedom."

The liberal policy of the Dutch regarding religion was a product of their historical experience. Having a Protestant majority, the Dutch fought an eighty-year war for their independence from Catholic Spain. In 1638 Ann Hutchinson (the daughter of a Puritan minister) was exiled from the Massachusetts Bay Colony. After a brief stay in Providence, she left for New Amsterdam. Hutchinson, her children and followers were killed by Indians north of New Amsterdam. Stuyvesant, a devoted member of the Dutch Reform Church, however, denied Lutherans and Catholics a right to establish their own churches.

In 1654, twenty-four (24) Sephardic Jews (of Spanish origin) arrived in New Amsterdam. A million Jews had once lived in Spain. With the defeat of the Moslems in Spain, Catholic monarchs Ferdinand and Isabelle ordered that Catholicism should be the only religion of Spain. In 1492 Jews were given the choice of conversion or exile. Many went to North Africa while others were welcomed into the Ottoman Empire. Many Conversos (converts to Christianity) practiced their Judaism in secret. Jews settled in Portugal until that state insisted upon conversion or exile; some emigrated to Portugal's colony of Brazil. When the Dutch seized Brazil during a war, many Jewish settlers openly returned to their faith. When Brazil was returned to Portugal, Jews who had been baptized but returned to Judaism were subject to a death penalty (public burning) for heresy. Some fled to Surinam, Dutch Guiana, while others sought refuge in New Amsterdam.

Peter Stuyvesant was no friend to the Jews. Stuyvesant wrote to the Dutch West India Company demanding their expulsion. His letter stated that the presence of the Jews was "very repugnant to the magistrates… owing to their present indigence they might become a public charge … hateful blasphemers of the name of Christ be not allowed to further infect and trouble this new colony." On April 26, 1655, he received a letter stating that Jews had fought bravely alongside the Dutch in

Brazil and that a number of Jews were shareholders in the Dutch West India Company. He was ordered "to let Jews remain provided the poor among them shall not become a public burden."

(https:en.wikipedia.org/wiki/Peter_Stuyvesant#Religious_freedom)

The British landed troops on Long Island in 1664 and received the surrender of the Dutch. New Netherlands was renamed New York. The Dutch were encouraged to remain and most were naturalized.

In France, wars of religion between Catholics and French Calvinists (Protestants) were brought to an end by the Edict of Nantes in 1598. It provided for tolerance and security for members of both Christian faiths. The revocation of the Edict by King Louis XIV led to the emigration of the French Protestants, who referred to themselves as Huguenots. New Rochelle bears the name given the town in New York settled by these French immigrants. New York's population was diverse. The census of 1790 noted its population being 340,120 people, 21,324 of whom were slaves and 4,654 persons of mixed race. New York had more slaves than any other northern state.

New Jersey

The Jerseys were separated from New York in 1664 and sold to two friends of the Duke of York, lords Berkley and Carteret. Not long afterward, the proprietors sold their interests to small groups of Quakers. In 1772 East and West Jersey were merged into single royal colony. Its population of 184,139 in the census of 1790 included English, Scotch-Irish, Welsh and Swedes Dutch, and Germans, a small number Sephardic Jews and 11,423 slaves.

Delaware

Delaware, located in the middle of England's colonies, had an interesting origin. One account is that a small group of Dutch settlers asked for the protection of Sweden in 1631. Sweden was a major European power in the 17th Century. In 1637, Swedish, Dutch and German investors created the New Swedish Company. In 1638, an expedition led by Peter Minuet (Governor of New Netherlands from 1626-31) established Fort Christina named for the Swedish Queen. Eight Hundred Swedes and Finns settled there. Following the seizure of a Dutch fort by the Swedes in 1654, Governor Stuyvesant sent five ships and 317 soldiers to seize New Sweden. The Swedes surrendered. Stuyvesant allowed them to remain and govern themselves. With the Dutch surrender of New Netherlands in 1664, Delaware became a British colony. The charter given to Pennsylvania reduced Delaware's size. The population of Delaware in 1790 was 59,094 including 8,887 slaves and 3,889 free "persons of color."

Pennsylvania

Pennsylvania's early immigration policy was shaped by William Penn, its proprietor. Penn was the son of Sir William Penn, the English Admiral who assisted Charles II monetarily. This was a deciding factor in William Penn's obtaining a charter in 1681. The charter made him the proprietor (the proprietor made the laws) over an area of 45,000 square miles. Penn called the area Sylvania (Latin for woods); it was the king who insisted that it be called Pennsylvania in memory of Penn's father.

William Penn had been a source of aggravation for his father. He joined the Society of Friends at the age of twenty-two and was arrested seven times. His book, *Sandy Foundations* challenged Anglican Church doctrines and led to his imprisonment in 1668. While in prison he wrote *No Cross, No Crown.* He praised religious diversity and condemned its suppression. The desire of the British government to be free of the Quakers might have been a second reason for chartering a colony for Quakers in America. As previously mentioned, Quakers defied the Church of England, refused to take oaths of loyalty, refused to serve in the military, were opposed to slavery and insisted upon their right to preach.

Penn lived in Pennsylvania from 1682-84. During that time, he completed a plan for the building of the city of Philadelphia (translated as city of Brotherly Love). He befriended the Lenape Indians, learned their dialects, negotiated a treaty and purchased land from them. His extending religious freedom to all who believed in God was the major factor in shaping immigration. Penn had once preached to Quakers in Germany. The Thirty Years Wars between Lutherans and Catholics was settled by requiring all residents to adopt either the Lutheran or Catholic faiths, depending upon the faith of the prince in whose domain they lived. Dissenting Mennonites, Anabaptists, as well as Lutherans and Catholics migrated. An estimated 65,000 migrated between 1727 and 1775. Most were poor and unable to afford their passage; two thirds came as indentured servants. Pennsylvania was referred to as "the best poor man's country." French Huguenots and Sephardic Jews settled in Pennsylvania. Its population in the census of 1790 was estimated to be 437,373 which included 3,737 slaves and 6,537 non-white free people.

Maryland

George Calvert, also known as Lord Baltimore, a Catholic nobleman served as Secretary of State to King Charles I. He advocated the establishment of a colony as a haven for Catholics in America. Upon his death, his son Cecil received a charter fto establish a proprietary colony in 1632. In defiance of England's established Anglican Church, King Charles I married Henrietta Maria a French Catholic princess. Maryland was named in honor of Henrietta Maria. Two hundred Roman Catholic Planters arrived to found the colony.

Aside from the original Catholic planters, the majority of the settlers in Maryland were Protestants. Lord Baltimore wrote to the king that "the greater part of the inhabitants of that province, three fourths at least consist of Protestants, Independents, Anabaptists, Quakers. Those of the Church of England and those of the Romish Church being fewest." In 1649, the year in which King Charles I was executed, Maryland adopted an Act of Toleration. It stated that residence in Maryland was open to all who believed in Jesus Christ and the Trinity. That was meant to reduce tensions between Protestant and

Catholic Christians. Most American history books, intent upon demonstrating the evolution of liberal ideas and tolerance in matters of religion generally end their discussion of Maryland by citing the act of toleration. That act, however, did not end religious conflict between Protestants and Catholics.

In May 1690, members of the Protestant Association overthrew the officers of the proprietor. In 1692, Maryland was declared a royal colony. Its changing status did not prevent the Protestant majority from enacting anti-Catholic legislation. A law in 1704 forbade Catholic priests from holding public services. In 1715, a tax was placed on the admission of each Irish immigrants in order "to prevent the too great importation of Papists." (Proper, 186) Two-years later a law was enacted denying Catholics the right to hold public office.

A unique feature in Maryland's immigration history is that more than 50,000 of its immigrants were convicts, sentenced to deportation for "felonious acts." A Maryland law during the proprietorship that imposed fines on persons who imported felons had been disallowed. An act of Parliament in 1717 that authorized the deportation of felons contributed to their number in Maryland. In 1755, a Maryland census noted that

Baltimore County alone had 472 male convicts over sixteen years of age, 87 female convicts over 16, 6 boys and 16 girls under 16. In total, the colony counted 1,509 convicts among its immigrants in a single year.

Maryland had more indentured servants than any other colony. The need for cheap labor led to the importation of enslaved Africans. The first slaves arrived in 1642. Maryland's population in the national census of 1790 was 319,000 of which 103,036 were slaves and 8,043 were free persons "of color."

The Carolinas

The English claim to the Carolinas was based upon the exploration of John Cabot, an Italian in the employ of England. In 1663, Charles II gave the lands in the Carolinas to William Berkley, George Carteret and Lord Clarendon to be governed as proprietary colonies. In 1665, settlers from Barbados established Albemarle County. The French Huguenots arriving in 1707 and German dissenters arriving in 1710 contributed to the diversity of the colony. Sephardic Jews, many of whom came from Barbados established a community in Charleston where they built "Bet Elohim" (House of God), one of the first synagogues in colonial America.

North Carolina is said to have developed with smaller farms devoted to producing tobacco. South Carolina developed large plantations which produced and exported rice, cotton and indigo. Historical accounts imply that South Carolina had a greater need for slave labor than its neighbor to the north. The census of 1790, however, notes that South Carolina had 107,000 slaves, and that contrary to popular belief, North Carolina had over 100,000.

In 1712, the proprietors recognized different interests of North Carolina and South Carolina and granted each the right to its own assembly. Riots and the expulsion of governors led proprietors to sell their interests to the Crown in 1729. Each colony was recognized as a separate royal colony.

As immigrants of European and African descent increased, the Native American population decreased. It is believed that twenty tribes inhabited the Carolinas. Small pox took its toll. Recognizing their systematic retreat, the Tuscarora and then the Yamassee and Creeks waged war against the colonists. They were decimated. The Tuscarora went north to join with the five nations of Iroquois Confederation in New York while the Yamassee settled in Spanish Florida.

The Census of 1790 recorded the population of North Carolina as containing 393,751 persons including 100,001 slaves and 4,975 non-white free people. South Carolina's population was 249,000 people including 107,014 slaves and 1,801 non-white free people.

Georgia

The establishment of Georgia in 1732 can be attributed to the vision and persistence of George Oglethorpe. A member of parliament, he had long advocated a colony where the indigent people (people without money) could begin life anew. The idea that Georgia would serve as a buffer between Spanish Florida into the Carolinas was an important factor in Oglethorpe's receiving a charter. The colony was named after King George II. An experiment, it was governed by twenty-one trustees, but Oglethorpe was its leader. Slavery and the drinking of alcohol was forbidden, the amount of land one could own was limited, and its plan required self-reliance rather dependence on imports and exports.

Savannah, its first settlement was a melting pot which included Puritans, Lutherans, and Quakers. Given the Catholic Spanish threat, Georgia was not welcoming to Catholics. Jews were originally banned, but when 43

Sephardic Jewish immigrants arrived in Savannah in 1733 Oglethorpe welcomed them.

The colony produced naval stores (pitch), rice and indigo. After Oglethorpe left, a petition to the assembly in 1649 requested that slavery be permitted. The petition was granted and large plantations developed. In 1752, the trustees refused to continue conducting the activities of the colony and Georgia became a royal colony. The national census of 1790 indicated that the population of Georgia was 82,584 of which 29, 264 were slaves and 368 were among the "all other free persons."

The *Georgia Encyclopedia* Identifies the following as part of Georgia's European population: lowland Scots, Lutheran Salzburgers, Rhineland Germans, French speaking Swiss, Irish convicts, some Piedmont Italians, and Russians. It notes that Sephardic Jews married Christian women and British men established "union with Creek females."
(https://www.georgiaencyclopedia.org/articles/history-archaeology/colonial-immigration)

Chapter 4 – The First Federal Immigration Laws

During the first decade of our nation's existence, Congress enacted three laws related to immigration and naturalization (the process by which a person of foreign birth, an alien, could become a citizen). **The Naturalization Act of 1790** (enacted on the 26th of March of that year) established the first "uniform rule" of naturalization. It stated, "Any alien being a free white person, who shall have resided (in the United States)....for the term of two years, may be admitted to become a citizen thereof." The color of the men writing the law is evident and their words at that time were meant to imply a difference between white and black. It is doubtful whether any thought was devoted to the possibility of Asians immigrating to the United States. The words "free white" would be a disturbing element in U.S. immigration policies for the next 150 years. In numerous Supreme Court decisions, those words would serve as justification for denying Chinese, Japanese and other Asians the right to become naturalized citizens.

The law stipulated that to be naturalized one had to demonstrate residency in a state for one year, live in the United States for two years and give proof "of good character." Upon promising to support the principles in the Constitution of the United States an oath could be administered and citizenship conferred in any common-law court. State justices rather than federal officials conferred citizenship. The law recognized children of U.S. citizens born outside of the United States as natural born citizens.

The Naturalization Act of January 25, 1795 repealed the Naturalization Act of 1790 and established more demanding conditions for naturalization. A person had to contact a court clerk and inform him of the intent to become a citizen three years before applying. One had to renounce loyalty to a specific prince or ruler and to name the state to which one had previously owed allegiance. One had to renounce any personal title previously recognized. One had to demonstrate residency in the United States for five years and satisfy the court that "he had behaved as a man of good moral character..." Citizenship continued to be reserved to white persons. The Naturalization Acts of 1790 and 1795 were enacted during the presidency of George Washington.

Angered that President Washington had declared neutrality in a war between Britain and France (after

France assisted the U.S. in its revolution), the French seized a number of U.S. vessels. While refusing to call for war, something called for by the members of the Federalist Party, President John Adams acceded to their call for greater internal security and the passage of the Alien and Sedition Acts. One act in the "package," was the Naturalization Act of 1798.

The **Naturalization Act of 1798** required a person to express one's intent to become a citizen five years before doing so, and to reside in the United States for fourteen years before being permitted to take the oath of loyalty and be granted citizenship. The act questioned the loyalty of new immigrants. Nativism, opposition by those already residing in the U.S. to specific new immigrant groups would be a recurrent development in our history.

The act also provided for the creation of an internal security system. Court clerks had to submit personal data – name, age, and nationality of all persons granted citizenship to the Department of State. All resident aliens were required to register after landing at an American port and to provide information regarding sex, place of birth, age, occupation and place of residence. In return, each was given a certificate of registry. Any alien who did not complete this requirement would be fined $2 and was subject to imprisonment. John Adams did not enforce this act.

One response to the **Naturalization Act of 1790** was the 'Federalist Riot of 1799." Four newly arrived immigrants posted signs in St. Mary's Catholic Church in Philadelphia calling for the repeal of the act. The congregation was torn. One priest called authorities and had the protesters arrested for causing a riot. A second priest testified that petitioning was common in churches in Ireland. A jury found "the rioters" innocent. (http://encyclopedia.densho.org/Naturalization_Act_of_ 1790/)

Presidents Washington and Adams, who supported those acts, were members of the Federalist Party. In 1800, Thomas Jefferson, a founder of the Democratic Republican Party was elected president. Jefferson was responsible for two important acts affecting immigration. **The Immigration Act of 1802** reduced the period known as the "notice time" during which one would indicate one's intent to seek citizenship from five to three years. It also reduced the years in which residency was required from fourteen to five. It directed officials in both state and territorial courts to confer citizenship and naturalize immigrants. Data on all incoming immigrants would be obtained by clerks at each port (name, place of birth, country of origin and intended place of settlement) and clerks were to issue certificates indicating their date of arrival. Noting the date of arrival would assist the alien seeking citizenship. (https://www.revolvy.com/page/Naturalization-Law-of-1802)

In his State of the Union Address to Congress in 1806, President Jefferson denounced the International Slave Trade as violating the human rights of the "long suffering …unoffending inhabitants of Africa." In 1807 Congress passed **An Act to Prohibit the Importation of Salves into any port or place within the Jurisdiction of the United States.** Going into effect in 1808 it forbade the importation of slaves into the United States. It did not outlaw the domestic slave trade, but nevertheless was a dramatic act by a president who continued to own slaves. A federal law passed in 1819 made engagement in the slave trade a capital offense. (http://avalon.law.yale.edu/19th_century/sl004.asp)

Two little known acts were the **Steerage Act of 1819** and the **Carriage Passenger Act of 1855**. Justified as acts to assure the health of incoming immigrants, they established regulations for travel. The act of 1819 stated that no more than two passengers could be carried for every five tons of the vessel. The act of 1855 was more specific. It required one passenger for every two tons, that there be 16 feet of clean deck for each passenger and stated that there could be no more than two tiers of births. There were no Federal laws limiting immigration into the United States at this time.

(https://en.wikipedia.org/wiki/Steerage_Act_of_1819)
(https://en.wikipedia.org/wiki/Carriage_of_Passengers_
Act_of_1855)

The **Treaty of Paris** which brought an end to the American Revolution recognized the Appalachian Mountains as the western border of the U.S. The purchase of Louisiana from France in 1815 doubled the size of the United States, extending its westward border to the Mississippi River; and included French speakers, both white and of mixed race who took pride in their Creole or Cajun culture. The acquisition of Florida from Spain in 1819 completed the north to south expansion along the eastern seaboard. Each territorial acquisition added to the ethnic diversity of the U.S.

(https://history.state.gov/milestones/1750-1775/treaty-
of-paris)

The victory of the United States in the Mexican War (1845-48) ended with the **Treaty of Guadalupe Hidalgo**. An estimated 80,000 Mexicans lived in the territories annexed by the United States. Those of

Mexican descent were given the choice of retaining Mexican citizenship or being recognized as U.S. citizens. Those who remained were promised citizenship, protection under our constitution and recognition of deeds to their land. They became citizens without being aliens or immigrants. Promises made to them were often unkept and acceptance as equals would prove elusive. One reason for Mexico's reluctance to prevent the present northward march of Central Americans through Mexico today may be a product of past resentment. A dramatic increase in U.S. population accompanied its territorial expansion.

(https://www.archives.gov/education/lessons/guadalupe-hidalgo)

Chapter 5 – The Second Wave

In the first census, the Census of 1790, the population of the United was estimated to be 3.9 million. The sixth census (a census being required every 10years) in 1840 reported the U.S. population reached 17, 069,000. The eighth census in 1860 reported the U.S. population had exceeded 31 million. The twenty-year period from 1840-1860 had seen the U.S. population grow by nearly 14 million, and the percentage of our population consisting of immigrants continued to grow.

Population and Foreign Born 1790 to 1849 Census Population, Immigrants per Decade				
Census	Population	Immigrants[1]	Foreign Born	%
1790	3,918,000	60,000		
1800	5,236,000	60,000		
1810	7,036,000	60,000		
1820	10,086,000	60,000		
1830	12,785,000	143,000	200,000 [2]	1.6%
1840	17,018,000	599,000	800,000 [2]	4.7%
1850	23,054,000	1,713,000	2,244,000	9.7%

1. The total number immigrating in each decade from 1790 to 1820 are estimates.

2. The number of foreign born in 1830 and 1840 decades are extrapolations.

(https://en.wikipedia.org/wiki/History_of_immigration_t o_the_United_States)

The two largest sources of immigration were Ireland and Germany, in that order. An estimated 1.6 million immigrants came from Ireland and 1.3 million came from Germany.

Population growth in Ireland had led to the repeated subdivision of land. British landlords increased rents for tenant farmers and evicted those unable to pay during the "great famine." A blight which killed the potato crop (upon which small farmers depended) began in 1845 and continued for a number of years. Almost one-million people died of starvation and disease and even more emigrated.

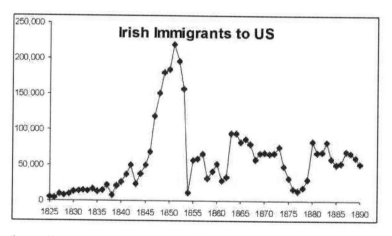

(https://www.pinterest.com/pin/574349758699725225/?autologin=true)

In New England, fear and hostility to Catholics had been demonstrated before the mass immigration of the Irish began. In 1834 mobs burned the Urseline Convent in Charlestown, Massachusetts, believing the tale that nuns had kidnapped young women and compelled them to join the nunnery. Most Irish who arrived after 1845 lacked capital and filled bottom rung jobs. Men were employed in building canals and later in laying track for railroads. In the city of Philadelphia women were employed in weaving. The Irish were 10% of the population of Philadelphia. One neighborhood, Kensington, was heavily Irish. Kensington was the target of the "Philadelphia Nativist Riots" (also called the Bible Riots) on May 6 and 8 and again on July 6 and 7, 1844 which destroyed Irish homes and property.

Catholic Irish were accused of being incapable of loyalty to the U.S. because of their loyalty to the pope. The American Republican Party called for the elimination of Catholics from American life. Members of Philadelphia labor unions feared the loss of jobs to Irish newcomers, and Irish pubs and wakes were repugnant to supporters of the temperance movement (opposed drinking of alcohol.) An immediate cause of rioting was the Catholic objection to using the Saint James version of the Bible (Protestant version) in public schools. In her essay, *Ethnic and Racial Conflict*, Marjorie Podolsky challenges the "romantic idea" that America was a "melting pot" in which new immigrants were embraced by old. She concludes that Nativism "has been a persistent theme in American history."

What would seem ironic to some was the role of Dennis Kearney, a naturalized Irish American who created the Workman's Party in San Francisco which demanded the exclusion of Chinese immigrants from California.

The second largest number of immigrants in the 1840's and 1850's came from Germany. German communities already dated back to the late 17th century. Mechanics and tradesmen settled in major cities while others went west and became farmers. Germans settled in Ohio, Wisconsin, the Dakotas and Texas. More than five million German immigrants settled in the U.S. before the end of the 19th century. Those who immigrated were later joined by relatives in what we now called chain migration. They were almost equally divided between Catholics and Lutherans. German Jews were a part of this German migration.

After the failure of the Revolution of 1848, German liberals who called themselves "forty-eighters" immigrated to the United States. Among them was the young revolutionary Karl Schurz who migrated with his family to Wisconsin. Shurz became a lawyer, a prominent Republican, a strong supporter of Lincoln, a Union general in the Civil War and later a Senator from Missouri. German immigration reached its high point as the U.S. in the 1880's.

(Bankston & Hidalgo, p. 288)

At the time of the American Revolution there were approximately 3,000 Jews in the U.S. Among the more than five million Germans who emigrated by 1880 were

300,000 German Jews. With few economic resources, many peddled goods to farm families from covered wagons along the western frontier. Jews settled in Paducah Kentucky, Cincinnati and San Francisco. Levi Strauss found success in making jeans for miners in California.

The 1870's witnessed the beginning of an influx of immigrants from Sweden. By 1880, 800,000 Swedish immigrants resided in the U.S. and more than 1.3 million emigrated by the second decade of the twentieth century. Swedish immigration was encouraged by population growth in Sweden and a shortage of good farm land. Arriving with some economic resources, most moved west to farmland in the midwest and Great Plains.

An interesting immigrant story is that of Joseph Pulitzer. Born into a Hungarian (Magyar) Jewish family, Pulitzer immigrated to the U.S. in 1864 at the age of 17. In Hungary he had received a good education. With his father's death and the accompanying economic hardship, he decided to emigrate. His passage was paid by military recruiters seeking soldiers for the civil war. Pulitzer served eight months in the Lincoln Cavalry. After the war, with little money, he boarded a freight train and made his way to St. Louis. He spoke German, French and Hungarian and found a place in the German speaking community. While working for the Atlantic and Pacific Railroad, its attorneys taught him the law. He was admitted to the bar at the age of 21. Because of his broken English he had few clients. Visiting the library in order to improve his English, he engaged in conversation with editors of the prominent German newspaper the *Westliche Post* who offered him the position of a reporter. One of its owners, Karl Schurz, became his model of what one could achieve in America. He is said to have worked sixteen hours a day and by 1872 had a controlling interest in the newspaper. In 1878 he purchased the *St.Louis Post Dispatch,* married Kate Davis in the Episcopal Church and was accepted in St. Louis society. He insisted that his newspaper was the champion of the common man. In 1883, already a wealthy man, he bought the *New York World* from Jay Gould. He marketed his newspaper as the newspaper of the masses.

(https://www.nps.gov/stli/learn/historyculture/pulitzer-in-depth.htm)

Pulitzer was aware that the Statue of Liberty was being sculptured in France as a gift to the American people. In 1885 the ship Isere landed at Bedloe's Island and deposited crates containing its parts. It could not be assembled because it lacked a pedestal. It sat in crates for over a year before it was erected in 1886. Using his newspaper, Pulitzer began a campaign that raised $100,000 for the Art Loan Fund from 120,000 people. The name of each contributor appeared in his newspaper, as did the sonnet solicited from Emma Lazarus by the chairman of the Art Fund. Emma Lazarus died in 1887 only one year after the statue was erected. Her sonnet *The New Colossus,* written in 1883 in anticipation of the arrival of the statue of liberty had nearly been forgotten. Rediscovered by a friend, its words were inscribed in a bronze plaque and placed in a wall in the pedestal of the statue in 1903. Its words reflected the pro-immigrant feelings of the people responsible for its inscription at that time:

…Mother of Exiles from her beacon-hand glows world-

wide

welcome her mild eyes command

…cries she with silent hope

Give me your tired, your poor, your silent masses

yearning to breathe free…

Send these the homeless, tempest tost to me

I lift my lamp behind the golden door.

Forces opposed to such sentiments and in favor of increased restriction were already gaining strength.

Using Pulitzer's endowment, Colombia University created a school of journalism in 1912.

Chapter 6 – California: An Immigration Battleground

Assuming a moral high ground in assisting undocumented immigrants in our own time, California's leaders may be consciously demonstrating their intent to break from their state's "checkered past."

On January 21, 1848 James W. Marshall found gold in California; thereafter its population grew geometrically. According to the census of 1850, California's population was 92,597; by 1860 it had reached 379,000, by 1870,560,000 and by 1880 its population was 864,594. The California gold rush inspired immigration and settlement.

California entered the Union as a "free state" in 1850 as part of the Compromise of 1850, opposing the expansion of slavery to California. This fact may lead one to assume that in taking the side of free-men "all was just in its world." More than any other state in the middle and late 1800's, California became a battleground in which some newcomers were welcomed while others were subjected to discriminatory laws and violence. Its policies would impact greatly upon the entire nation.

In 1850, California's Native American (Indian tribal) population was 150,000. By 1860, it was 30,000. Invasion by rapacious miners and settlers left the Native American tribes near to starvation. Indian raids were followed by their near destruction from attacks by miners and the state militia.

"Californos," the Mexican inhabitants in California before it was lost to the United States in the Mexican War (1845-48) had been promised in the Treaty of Guadalupe Hidalgo that titles to their land would be respected. The "informality" of Mexico's land grants allowed miners and settlers to lay claim to their land. Bankruptcy, due to legal costs, took its toll even among those with strong claims. Most eventually lost their land.
(https://www.archives.gov/education/lessons/guadalupe-hidalgo)

The announcement that Gold had been found at Sutter's Mill in 1848 led to a Gold Rush (1848-55) which brought immigrants to California from all over the world. Among the first to flood into California were Latin Americans from Chile, Panama and Mexico. Many had crossed the Isthmus of Panama and made their way to California. The California legislature imposed "a foreign miner's tax" requiring persons who were not

American citizens to pay a monthly license fee in order to retain their claims. A fee as high as $20 a month drove most of them from their claims. African American families numbering between 2,000 and 3,000 came to California. Laws were enacted to racially segregate their children in public schools and they were denied the right to testify in court. Arbitrary claims by those pretending to enforce Federal Fugitive Slave Laws kept "Free Negroes" on edge.
(http://ohiohistorycentral.org/w/Fugitive_Slave_Law_of_1850)

Word of the gold rush in California reached Asia, and immigration by Chinese and Japanese immigrants would follow. The immigration of Asians would be a source of some of most bitter race driven conflicts in our nation's history.

Chinese began arriving in California in 1851. China had been defeated in the first Opium War (1839-42), a war caused by Britain's insistence that it be allowed to sell opium in China. The Taiping Rebellion (1850-64) was raging and floods and famine encouraged thoughts of emigration. The first to come were mostly young peasants from Canton. They hoped to find gold and return to China. Most had their passage paid by merchants whom they had promised to repay with their earnings. They referred to this as "credit tickets." Unlike contract labor, those who immigrated were not committed to work for any specific individual. With the passage of the Contract Labor Law this distinction would be ignored. Some Chinese provoked animosity in being able to operate abandoned claims at a marginal profit. Race was the distinguishing factor. The ease in identifying Chinese made them easy targets of the Foreign Miner's Tax. Driven from the mines some opened restaurants and businesses that supplied the basic needs of miners. Others found work laying down track for the Central Pacific Railroad.

Anti-Chinese sentiment and violence was evident from the time of their arrival. Dennis Kearney organized the Workingman's Party in 1877 to oppose Chinese immigration. The Sandlot Riots in San Francisco in that same year began with workingmen shouting "the Chinese must go." The rampage which lasted a number of days resulted in the deaths of 19 men, women and children. California was not alone in witnessing anti-Chinese violence. Chinatowns, established in mining and railroad towns experienced violence in many states.

Great effort was devoted to formulating laws meant to drive out Chinese and dissuade future Chinese immigrants. The Foreign Miner's Tax was followed by a law in 1854 that denied them the right to testify in court. In 1862 they were required to pay a police tax. A California law in 1879 prohibited municipalities and corporations from employing Chinese, and a state law in 1880 forbid inter-racial marriage. Each of these laws preceded the federal **Chinese Exclusion Act of 1882**. (http://ocp.hul.harvard.edu/immigration/exclusion.html)

In 1868, Secretary of State William Seward believed it would be advantageous to have good diplomatic relations with China. He sent Aaron Burlingame to China where he negotiated the Burlingame-Seward Treaty. The treaty provided for the free immigration and travel by citizens of each nation to the other. Under domestic pressure, the treaty was re-negotiated, and China conceded the right of the U.S. to regulate immigration but not to suspend it.

Recognizing that the federal government had the power to regulate immigration and naturalization, the California delegation took the lead in advancing the passage of federal laws that would deter Chinese immigration. **The Immigration Law of 1870** made it illegal to import Chinese, Japanese or Mongolian prostitutes. This law made it difficult for any single woman in China to obtain

a visa to travel to the United States. The American Consul in Hong Kong was given the task of deciding which Chinese women were married and which might be rejected for being of low moral character. Single female applicants for visas had to provide extensive information about their families and were subjected to medical examinations to determine whether they were morally upright. In 1877 of hundreds of women who applied for visas only 77 were admitted. Laws criminalizing marriage between Chinese and Caucasians were enacted in California and many other states.
(https://en.wikipedia.org/wiki/Naturalization_Act_of_18 70)

The immigration laws of 1790 and 1795 restricted naturalization to free white males. The distinction was made with Africans in mind. Chinese and Japanese were never subjects of consideration. An irony lay in the fact that children born in the U.S. of Chinese parentage were citizens by definition (the fourteenth amendment stated that anyone born in the U.S. was a citizen of the U.S.) while their parents were not. In 1888, the U.S. Supreme Court ruled that any child born in the U.S. was a citizen.

In 1882, Congress passed the **Chinese Exclusion Act**. It began. "Whereas in the opinion of the Government of the United States the coming of Chinese laborers to this country endangers the good order of certain localities…..the coming of Chinese laborers to the United States…is hereby suspended." The term of the act was ten years. Exempted from its provisions were Chinese laborers in the U.S. prior to 1880, diplomats on business and household servants. A ship captain bringing Chinese laborers to the U.S. was threatened with the confiscation of his vessel. A Chinese person travelling outside of the U.S. was required to obtain a certificate that would facilitate re-entry. The **Scott Act** in 1888 denied reentry to those who traveled outside of the United States.

(https://www.ourdocuments.gov/doc.php?flash=true&doc=47)

(https://www.revolvy.com/topic/Scott%20Act%20(1888)&item_type=topic)

In 1892 the **Geary Act** introduced by California congressman Thomas Geary affirmed the ban on Chinese laborers and added new provisions. It prohibited the use of Habeas Corpus by Chinese already in the United States. They could not bear witness in court nor be released upon bail. The law required them to register, carry documents and provide proof of their eligibility to remain in the U.S. or face deportation. In 1893, the **McCreary Act** expanded the definition of a laborer to include fishermen, miners, laundry men and merchants.

(http://immigrationtounitedstates.org/514-geary-act-of-1892.html)

(http://www.chinesefamilyhistory.org/exclusion-acts.html)

A legal challenge by a Chinese resident to his being denied the right to naturalization arose in the case of Fong Yue Ting v. U.S. in 1893. The petitioner applied for a certificate of residency in New York County. His argument was that he had resided in the U.S. before the Chinese Exclusion Act and was entitled to do so. The clerk would not accept the testimony of another Chinese and demanded a Caucasian witness which the petitioner did not have. Upon appeal the case reached the U.S. Supreme Court. The majority opinion of Justice Gray denied the petition. His opinion read, "…every sovereign nation has the power…to forbid the entrance of foreigners within its boundaries…the exercise of which can be invoked for the maintenance of its absolute independence and security."

(https://supreme.justia.com/cases/federal/us/130/581/case.html)

In 1913 California enacted a law denying the right to own land to anyone who was ineligible to become a citizen. Census statistics indicate a decline the Chinese population from 100,000 in the U.S. in 1890 to 61, 639 in 1920.

The Chinese Exclusion Act was repealed in 1943 when China and the United States were allied against Japan. (https://history.state.gov/milestones/1937-1945/chinese-exclusion-act-repeal)

The first Japanese arrived in 1871. There were 1360 Japanese in the U.S. in 1890. In 1898 the U.S. won the Spanish American war and gained control of the Philippines. In order to establish a naval base between the continental U.S. and the Philippines, the U.S. annexed Hawaii in 1898. Prior to annexation, Hawaiian sugar growers had recruited labor from Japan. When the U.S. annexed Hawaii, 60,000 Japanese in Hawaii became eligible to enter the United States.

After the passage of the Chinese Exclusion Act, the Issei, first generation Japanese were recruited for labor on the railroads. They helped build the Great Northern and Northern Pacific Railroads. (archive.vancouver.wsu.edu). They made up almost half of Oregon's railroad labor force in 1907. In Portland a Japanese association provided housing and advised newcomers on employment opportunities in fishing canaries, saw mills and farming. Most Issei had farming backgrounds. Unable to buy land because of discrimination they leased land. Japanese were driven out of towns in Idaho.

In 1900, 25,000 Japanese lived in the U.S. In 1905, the year in which 17,000 Japanese immigrants arrived in California, the Asian Exclusion League was created. In 1906, there were assaults on Japanese and a boycott of their restaurants in San Francisco. The creation of a racially segregated public school track for Japanese children (in addition to colored and white) by the Board of Education in San Francisco became an international incident. Japan complained that a treaty between the U.S. and Japan for mutual free entry had been violated. At this time President Theodore Roosevelt was negotiating the Treaty of Portsmouth to end the war between Japan and Russia. Roosevelt appealed to the members of the San Francisco school board to reverse its decision and they did so. In 1908, the United States and Japan negotiated the **Gentleman's Agreement**. The agreement involved compromise. Japan agreed to withhold passports from Japanese laborers, while the U.S. agreed to allow wives, children and close relatives of Japanese already in the U.S. to join them. A surge of Japanese immigration in the next twenty years increased the Japanese population to 100,000.

By 1915, 450 residents of Japanese birth had been naturalized. When Takao Ozawa petitioned for naturalization in 1915 and was denied, he appealed to the U.S. Supreme Court. Ozawa was born in Japan but lived in the U.S. with his wife and two children for more than twenty years. As early as 1902 he had filed a letter of intent to seek citizenship. He spoke English and was employed by an American company. Rather than argue against the injustice in the Immigration Law of 1790 that stated that naturalization was reserved to white persons, he argued that hat his skin was as light as that of white persons. The Supreme Court rejected his appeal. Writing for a unanimous court, Justice George Sutherland wrote, "...the words 'white person' was meant to indicate only a person of what is popularly known as the Caucasian race." Sutherland stated that Japanese were not commonly considered white persons, and he added, "...we should not at this late day feel at liberty to disturb it." The decision of the court was withheld while diplomatic discussion with Japan over limiting of naval forces in the Pacific was taking place. The decision of the Supreme Court was handed down on November 13, 1922. (Densho Encyclopedia:

(http://encyclopedia.densho.org/Ozawa_v._United_States/)

Three months later Justice Sutherland wrote a similar majority opinion in the case of United States v. Bhagat. Bhagat Singh was a Sikh immigrant claiming to be of high Caste (indicating his light-colored skin) in India. The Supreme Court decision held that he too was not a "free white" person as required by the Naturalization Law of 1790.

Chapter 7 – The Federal Footprint Grows

The United States received 788,992 immigrants in 1882, the largest number of immigrants in any single year in its history. Congress responded by passing both the **Chinese Exclusion Act** and the **Immigration Act of 1882**. A pattern of restriction meant to reduce the numbers of immigrants would follow.

The **Immigration Act of 1882** created the framework for complete federal control of immigration. The Immigration Act of 1882 was signed into law on August 3, 1882, three months after the passage of the **Chinese Exclusion Act**. To assure the funding of an administrative bureaucracy a head tax of fifty cents was required or each incoming immigrant; it went into an "immigration fund." The head tax would be raised to $8 in 1917 which in some cases would make it prohibitive. The act established categories of persons to be excluded and denied admission to the U.S. by federal inspectors. Among those initially ecluded were convicts, lunatics, idiots and "any person unable to take care of himself or herself without becoming a public charge."
(http://immigrationtounitedstates.org/585-immigration-act-of-1891.html)

In response to the demands of labor organizations and the belief that contract labor provided a vehicle for Chinese immigration, Congress enacted the **Contract Law of 1885**. The law stated, "It shall be unlawful for any person, company, partnership or corporation…to pre-pay the transportation (of persons) …to perform labor or service of any kind in the United States." (https://en.wikipedia.org/wiki/Alien_Contract_Labor_La w#The_Law)

Excused from exclusion were professionals, actors, artists and domestic servants. The law in 1887 placed enforcement under the control of the Secretary of the Treasury and the Treasury Department.

The **Immigration Act of 1891** was more restrictive that than of 1882. Prior to this act ports were controlled locally. While the Treasury Department was empowered to supervise immigration, it was customary for that department to consult with governors of states who recommended personnel to be employed. The act of 1891 required oversight by federal officials. They were required to inspect ports and vessels. The Office of Superintendent of Immigration was created. Officers would establish control points on the Canadian and Mexican borders. Added to the categories of persons to be excluded were insane people, polygamists, epileptics and people with contagious diseases. The Office of the Superintendent would hear appeals from immigrants. Federally controlled inspection stations were established at points of entry.

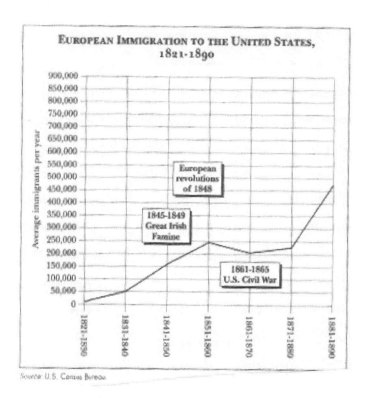

(Bankston & Hidalgo, p. 237)

Immigration stations where inspections would take place were established in New York City, Gloucester (N.J.), Boston, Miami, Buffalo (N.Y.), Detroit, New Orleans, Seattle, San Francisco, San Juan, and Honolulu. The two most important immigration inspection stations were Ellis Island in New York Harbor and Angels Island in San Francisco Bay.

A reception center for immigrants had been created as a joint project between New York City and New York State at Castle Garden, a location at the tip of Manhattan before the creation of a federal inspection center on Ellis Island. Serving immigrants from 1855 until 1890, its purpose was primarily to assist immigrants. It was a place where an immigrant could exchange foreign currency for U.S. dollars, buy railroad tickets for locations far and wide and be given information about jobs and housing. The purpose of the newer federal inspection center on Ellis Island would be the exclusion of "undesirables."

The construction of the Ellis Island Immigration Station began in 1890 and was completed in 1892. It contained twelve buildings, a hospital, restaurant and kitchen. Those who traveled to America on steamships could travel first class (private up-scale accommodations), second class (middle grade accommodations) or steerage (an area below the first two decks lined with bunks). It was assumed that persons in the upper decks were better off economically, so inspections were generally confined to people who traveled in steerage.

When a ship came into the harbor doctors and inspectors went to meet it. People with contagious diseases were sent to hospitals in New York City. Doctors quarantined people whom they suspected of having problems with hearing or speech. Persons suspected of having a problem were marked across the shoulder with chalk (CT-trachoma, H-heart problem, X for mental illness.) Officials drew conclusions about a person's fitness by observing whether an immigrant was having difficulty carrying his suitcase up a flight of stairs. Difficulty could be seen as an impediment to his being an independent and self-sustaining person.

It is estimated that 12 million immigrants passed through this 3.3 acre inspection station on Ellis Island. The majority of those inspected were Italians, Jews, Hungarians, Greeks, Czechs, Serbs, Armenians and Turks. An estimated 5,000 people passed through on a normal day. Its busiest day was April 17, 1907 when 11,747 immigrants passed through its gates. It is estimated that 40% of all U.S. citizens entered through Ellis Island. Only 2% who passed through Ellis Island were deported, but this amounted to a quarter of a million people.

Ellis Island could be a place of joy and tears. One account preserved was of a father, judged too ill to be admitted, who was permitted to see his son one last time at the gate of Ellis Island before being sent back to Europe.
(https://www.loc.gov/exhibits/haventohome/haven-haven.html)

Women under 16 and children generally had to await the arrival of a relative who would come to meet them. The **Immigration Acts of 1921 and 1924** would dramatically reduce the number of people who went through Ellis Island and would ultimately render it unnecessary. Beginning in 1924 a Consular System was established. By 1931, almost all immigrants were evaluated in ports from which they sailed before being granted a visa by a U.S. consular official.
(http://immigrationtounitedstates.org/589-immigration-act-of-1921.html)

(https://history.state.gov/milestones/1921-1936/immigration-act)

Construction of the inspection station on Angel's Island in San Francisco Bay began in 1905 and was completed in 1910. Sometimes called "the Ellis Island of the West," it was designed primarily to control the flow of Chinese after the passage of the Chinese Exclusion Acts. Only in 1915 did Japanese immigration exceed that of Chinese. Immigrants from 84 nations went through its portals including Indians and Filipinos

An interesting dilemma resulted from the San Francisco Earthquake of 1906. All records related to births, death and immigration were destroyed. Chinese residents insisted that they had acquired citizenship and their claims were generally accepted. The Constitution of the U.S. states that children of American citizens, though born abroad are citizens of the U.S. Large numbers of Chinese in China claimed to be children of these citizens, and with papers in hand made efforts to gain admission. Inspectors questioned arrivals in specific terms and deported "paper fathers," "papers mothers" and "paper sons." These were people who presented papers showing descent from a person born in the U.S. and entitled to citizenship in the U.S. The average detention was two to three weeks. The longest was 22 months. At Angels Island 18% of arrivals were rejected. Poems inscribed by detainees were copied from its walls in the 1930's. One poem read,

America has power, but not justice.

In prison, we were victimized as if we were guilty

Given no opportunity to explain, it was really brutal

I bow my head in reflection

But there is nothing I can do.

(https://sites.google.com/site/donslibrary/Home/united-states-fiction/the-poems-of-angel-island)

Chapter 8 – Increased Demands for Restriction

Years	# of Immigrants	
1841-1850	1,713,251	
1851-1860	2,598,214	
1861-1870	2,314,325	
1871-1880	2,812,191	
1881-1890	5,246,613	It included one million Germans
1891-1900	3,687,584	
1901-1910	8,795,386	Two million Italians – peak of Italian immigration 17,000 Japanese entered from Hawaii in 1905 485,000 Jews entered in 1910

(http://www.emmigration.info/us-immigration-history-statistics.htm)

By the turn of the twentieth century the United States was being recognized as a world power. Its agricultural and industrial development had been fed by immigration. The table on the previous page indicate numbers of immigrants in each decade leading up to the presidency of Theodore Roosevelt:

Important immigration policies were adopted during the presidency of Theodore Roosevelt (1901-09). Roosevelt became president after the assassination of President William McKinley in Buffalo on September 6, 1901. McKinley was shot by Leon Czolgosz, son of a Polish immigrant and an admitted anarchist who saw the president as a symbol of oppression. The **Immigration Act of 1903,** signed into law by Roosevelt, was also called the **Anarchist Exclusion Act.**
(http://immigrationtounitedstates.org/586-immigration-act-of-1903.html)

Anarchism was an angry response to what was perceived as oppression by autocratic governments. Believing that governments controlled by capitalists were naturally oppressive; anarchists favored both the destruction of capitalism and oppressive governments. Believing that freedom was possible only in small communistic communities they embraced revolutionary violence as a means of change. Among the "Forty-Eighters" who left

Germany after the failure of the Revolution of 1848 were people who were anarchists. Johan Most, a German anarchist who immigrated to the U.S. in 1882 published the newspaper *Freiheit* (Freedom). His book *Free Society* called for the formation of revolutionary committees, violent revolution, and abolition of private property. Just as he had praised the assassination of Czar Alexander II of Russia, his response to the murder of President McKinley was that it was normal to kill a leader.

In 1886 what began as a pro-labor rally protesting the shooting of workers at the Harvester factory in Chicago became a scene of bloodshed when a bomb was thrown at police. In what came to be called the Haymarket Affair, four labor leaders were accused, convicted and hanged for inciting the bomb thrower. The four were of German extraction who were said to have been anarchists. The bomber was never found.
(https://en.wikipedia.org/wiki/Johann_Most)

The Immigration Act of 1903 added four new classes of immigrants to be excluded from admission to the United States: anarchists, beggars, epileptics and people involved with prostitution (prostitutes and procurers). Other than what could be observed, it is hard to conceive of questions which would have resulted in responses leading to the exclusion of an anarchist. Another act signed by the president made an ability to communicate in the English language a requirement for naturalization.

Among the immigrants who came to the United States between 1880 and 1920 were an estimated 4 million Italians, 2.5 million Jews (from the Russian and Austrian-Hungarian Empires), 1.7 million Poles, 500,000 Hungarians, 100,000 Armenians and 300,000 Greeks. In 1903, 857,046 immigrants entered the U.S. and one million entered in 1905. The census of 1910 indicated that 747,000 English speaking Canadians, 440,000 French speaking Canadians and 720,000 Mexicans had settled in the U.S. There is an absence of data indicating how many returned home.

Italians and Jews accounted for the largest numbers of immigrants from southern and eastern Europe during the "wave of immigration" between 1880 and 1910. 12,000 foreign born Italians lived in New York City in 1880, and their numbers increased to 341,000 in 1910. While only 14,000 foreign born Jews lived in New York City in 1880, their numbers increased to 484,000 in 1910. (Foner, p. 10)

Writers of sensational newspaper and magazine articles, whom Theodore Roosevelt called "muckrakers" highlighted overcrowding, poverty and crime in the new ethnic neighborhoods. "Progressive writer," Jacob Riis, a reporter and an immigrant from Denmark, was the author of *Battle with the Slum (1902) and Children of the Tenements (1902).* While Riis was an advocate of additional governmental assistance to alleviate undesirable conditions, advocates of restricting immigration used his accounts as evidence that the new ethnic neighborhoods threatened the very existence of the nation.

In 1907, Congress established a joint House-Senate committee to study the effects of immigration on the United States. Its chairman was William Paul Dillingham of Vermont. Dillingham and most of the members of his commission were in favor of dramatically restricting immigration. With congressional funding, Dillingham employed teams of "social scientists" to conduct research. The committee's strongest supporter in the Senate was Henry Cabot Lodge of Massachusetts. The Commission compiled 42 volumes containing its research and conclusions between 1907 and 1911. Its findings provided the rationale for the restrictive acts of the 1920's.

Dillingham began his research in Europe in 1907. He divided his nine-member research team and directed its members to study the people in the nations from which a majority of immigrants were coming. Members of the team confined their first study to Italy, Austria-Hungary, Russia and Greece. After Charles Darwin's theory of evolution was introduced, schools of thought arose which contended that human beings of different races were at different levels of evolution, superior and inferior. Dillingham "scientists" noted the hair, shape of the head, and "psychic disposition" of those studied. Among their conclusions was that Slavs were fanatical about religion, while Jews had a propensity to live in urban areas and incorporated many of the "Shylock types." Italians were described as excitable and impulsive with little ability to function in organized society.

Accounts noted that 47 Italian "banks" found ways of sending remittances back to relatives in Italy while 15 such "banks" were run by Jews. It was noted that this siphoned off American money. Schools were studied and teachers questioned about their children. A conclusion was that 63.9 % of Italian children were retarded, while 66.9% of Jewish children of Polish origin were retarded. These two ethnic groups provided the largest number of immigrants from southern and Eastern Europe. Studies showing that more Irish and Germans suffered from mental illness than immigrants from southern and Eastern Europe were discarded as were studies showing that people from Northern and Western Europe were as dependent upon public assistance as new immigrants. Three volumes were devoted to the study of the Japanese and "other immigrant races."

On December 1, 1910, Dillingham appeared before the North American Civil League in Boston to advocate restriction. His conclusion was that "...rural Anglo-Saxon Americans were threatened by hordes of southern and Eastern Europeans who populated the teeming cities." A bill passed in Congress to make literacy a condition for admission but was vetoed by President Taft.
(www.uvm.edu/-hag/histreview/vol6/lund.html)

The forty-one volumes produced by the Dillingham Commission were viewed as more important than any previous report on the effects of immigration. They were used to justify the increasingly restrictive immigration policies of 1917, 1921 and 1924. A Harvard study states that "They concluded that immigration from southern

and eastern Europe posed a serious threat to American society and culture and should therefore be greatly reduced."
(http://ocp.hul.harvard.edu/immigration/dillingham.html)

An important factor influencing the way Dillingham Commission conducted its study was the credibility accorded the "science" of Eugenics. The publication of *The Origin of the Species by Process of Natural Selection* by Charles Darwin in 1859 impacted dramatically upon prevailing scientific thought. In his *Theory of Evolution*, Darwin wrote of simple life forms, "social Darwinists" almost immediately applied his suppositions to human societies. Wealth and power were attributed to superior genes, while poverty was attributed to genetic inferiority. In an age of imperialism (the 19th and early 20th) the ability of some nations to create empires was attributed to racial superiority.

Eugenics, as a science embraced the idea of evolution affecting human development. Among its assumptions was that not all humans had evolved to the same extent and there were the genetically superior and inferior. "Progressive Era (c.1901-1921)" thinkers concluded that information gleaned through this science gave man the power to regulate human interaction and produce superior human beings. Eugenics was considered an important school of scientific reasoning at the turn of the twentieth century. The Carnegie and Rockefeller Foundations and the Harriman family funded eugenic schools in the U.S. and Europe (preference being given to Germany). Columbia University anthropology professor Franz Boaz insisted that the study of human skulls revealed the place of families of humans in the process of evolution. Biologist Charles B. Davenport, active in the American Breeders Association, founded the Eugenics Record Office in Cold Springs Harbor New York in 1911 and strongly supported immigration restriction.

Eugenics was embraced by many members of the medical profession and became a basis for the passage of sterilization laws in the United States. A North Carolina law allowed social workers to recommend sterilization for those judged to have IQs of lower than 70. California took the lead in sterilization. It is estimated that more than 64.000 Americans were forcibly sterilized in the U.S. between 1890 and 1924.
(https://en.wikipedia.org/wiki/Eugenics_in_the_United_S tates)

The Immigration Restriction League, having among its founders Harvard graduates in Boston, took the position that sexual relations between persons of Anglo-Saxon origin with those of less evolved races would produce an inferior racial type.

In his book *Strangers in the Land,* John Higgins attributes the growth of race-based nativism to the elite members of old New England families. He writes, "the race-thinkers were men and women who rejoiced in their colonial ancestry...racist nativists worshipped tradition....and in the tumult of the nineties it seemed to them that everything....sacred was threatened with dissolution." (Higgins, p. 139)

Racial discrimination was a part of the American mindset since the colonial period. The end of slavery was followed by racial segregation. The U.S. Supreme Court upheld the constitutionality of racial segregation laws in its decision in the case of Plessy v Ferguson in 1896. President Woodrow Wilson extended racial segregation to every department of the executive branch of the national government. As portrayed in the contemporary movie *Hidden Figures,* separate toilets for white and colored employees existed in government agencies. In 1924 Virginia would pass its Racial Integrity Law with its "one drop rule." One drop of African blood excluded a person from the white race.

Immigration laws cannot be understood without an understanding of society at the time of their passage. (http://www2.vcdh.virginia.edu/lewisandclark/students/projects/monacans/Contemporary_Monacans/racial.html) In the years, just prior to World War I, anti-immigration lobbies such as the American Protective Association (established in 1887) and the Immigration Restriction League (founded in Boston in 1894) were laying a foundation for the most restrictive immigration policies in our history. Nine million immigrants entered the U.S. in the first decade of the twentieth century. Seventy percent of the immigrants entering the U.S. in that decade were from southern and eastern Europe. World War I began in July 1914 and immigration declined sharply. "Restrictionists" did not relent in their efforts to limit immigration. They argued that a massive inflow would resume after the war and they secured the passage of the **Immigration Act of 1917**. The **Immigration Act of 1917**, also called the **Literacy Test Act** was passed by Congress but was vetoed by President Wilson on December 14, 1916. Congress overrode his veto and it became law on February 6, 1917.

The passage of the Immigration Law of 1917 preceded the entrance of the U.S. into World War I on April 6, 1917. That law addressed a number of issues. It added to the category of persons who might be excluded persons defined as mentally defective, persons with constitutional psychopathic inferiority (terminology applied to suspected homosexuals), epileptics, alcoholics, political radicals, polygamists, prostitutes and vagrants.

Most significant was that it barred immigrants over the age of 16 who were illiterate. Immigrants were required to demonstrate an ability to read and write in their own language. Many who came from peasant backgrounds in Greece, Italy or the Russian Empire before World War I were illiterate. The raising of the head tax to $8 was meant to deter "undesirables." A final element was its declaration of America as an Asia Free Zone. While Japanese and Filipinos were excluded from this provision, the act barred the admission of all other Asians into the United States. It was referred to in the small Indian American community (people from India) as the Indian Exclusion Act. The Immigration Act of 1917 was the first act in what would later become "a perfect storm" and serve to restrict immigration to the United States from Europe.

An exception to the restrictionist sentiment was the passage of the Jones-Shafroth Act on March 2, 1917, which gave native-born Puerto Ricans United States citizenship.

Chapter 9 – "The Perfect Storm"

Restricting the immigration of "less desirable" Europeans became possible because of what may be described as a perfect storm. Events conspired to produce an atmosphere in which groups opposed to restriction found themselves a minority.

The United States entered World War I in April 1917. President Wilson believed in the need for total mobilization. He understood that not all Americans would support it. The Espionage Act enacted in June 1917 was meant to prevent dissent by people of Germanic, Austro-Hungarian, and Irish backgrounds and by socialists who denounced it as a war waged for profits by capitalists. To mobilize public opinion in favor of the war, by executive order he established the Committee on Public Life (CPL) under the chairmanship of George Creel. Creel had been a journalist for the *Denver Post* and *Rocky Mountain News.* Describing its purposes as informational and educational, the committee vilified foreign enemies, encouraged enlistment, produced exaggerated accounts of American heroism and "defined" Americanism. One hundred percent Americanism became a rallying cry. Seventy-five thousand people were employed in disseminating and controlling the flow of information through posters, radio and documentary films. Negative perceptions of Europeans as well as an increased awareness of how to shape public opinion remained after the committee ceased to function in 1919.

Nearly 117,000 Americans died in World War I. President Wilson attended the peace conference at Versailles. Once Germany surrendered, the victors (Britain, France, Italy) awarded themselves reparations from Germany, divided its colonies and awarded themselves control of regions that had formerly been parts of the Ottoman Empire. Wilson won the pledge to create a League of Nations. Despite a national tour to pressure the Senate to ratify the Treaty of Versailles, the Senate refused to do so. Americans rejected the idea that they would be called upon to defend the borders of newly created European states as required by the treaty. The idea that we had sacrificed so that European victors could benefit led to a new isolationism.

Two million men had been sent to Europe. Their return to civilian life led to the economic "depression of 1920-1921." Unemployment, initially at 12% in 1920 declined to 6.7% in 1921 and 2.4% in 1923. Though brief in duration, that temporary depression lent itself to the support of the position by organized labor that mass immigration would bring down wages and endanger the livelihood of Americans.

Owners of American industry, manufacturers and builders were usually opposed to restriction. Many employers were convinced that Labor unrest was driven by immigrants with radical ideologies. Out of a sense of patriotism workers had accepted lower wages and were reluctant to strike during the war. The demands of labor for high wages after the war led to many strikes across the nation. On January 21, 1919, 35,000 shipyard workers in Seattle affiliated with the Metal Trades Council went on strike. Another 14,000 joined the strike in Tacoma. Unions joined together and conducted what appeared to be a general strike for five days. Shipyard workers continued their strike for longer. At the end the unions voted to end the strike. Aware of the Bolshevik Revolution in Europe, some newspapers attributed strikes by American workers to foreign influence.

The danger attributed to aliens was reinforced by a series of bombings by anarchists. In April 1919, 36 packaged bombs were found in the General Post Office in New York City. Bombs meant to explode on May 1, 1919, the anniversary of the Haymarket bombing, were sent to editors and government officials. Some thought it part of a Bolshevik conspiracy.

On June 2, 1919, at the same hour, bombs went off in New York, Boston, Cleveland, Washington, Philadelphia and Patterson, New Jersey. They are believed to have been sent by the followers of Luigi Galleani an Italian immigrant and anarchist who arrived in the U.S. in 1901. Settling first in Patterson, New Jersey, Galleani published *La Questione Sociali,* the leading Italian anarchist periodical which denounced Socialists for being non-violent. Relocating to an Italian community in Vermont, he published *Cronaca Sovversiva (*Subversive chronicle). That publication listed the names and locations of "enemies of the people." Packages were sent to Seattle Mayor Henson and to Justice Oliver Wendell Holmes. Holmes had written the majority opinion in the Supreme Court case upholding the conviction of Charles Schenck (leader of the American Socialist Party) whose fliers urged draftees not to serve. A bomb also blew up at the home of Attorney General Mitchell Palmer. After Galleani's deportation in 1919, his followers are believed to have planted the bomb that exploded on September 16, 1920 opposite Wall Street, killing thirty-eight people and wounding two hundred. Whether the suppositions were true is less important than what people believed, and those beliefs supported the demand for increased restrictions.

Between November 1919 and January 1920 Attorney General Mitchell Palmer conducted what are remembered as "the Palmer raids." On January 2, 1920 raids were conducted by government agents in thirty cities. Between 3,000 and 10,000 aliens and "radicals" were arrested. Those arrested were accused of being radicals, anarchists, socialists and communists. More than 500 were deported without due process of law. The names of 1600 "radical" immigrants were given to Secretary of Labor Louis Post (the Labor Department was then in charge of enforcing immigration laws). More than 70% of the deportation orders were reversed.

The absence of strong opposition to restriction was the result of a nearly perfect storm. Old stock New Englanders in favor of restriction found support from the advocates of Eugenics. Industrial workers feared the lowering of wages, while employers feared increased radicalism. Finding themselves confined by racial segregation in the south, many African Americans responded to a need for labor in the north during World War I. African American leaders may have feared racist ideologues, but they also feared that black workers would be replaced by immigrants and many supported restrictions. At the other end of the spectrum, opposing an influx of Catholics and Jews was the Ku Klux Klan.

Chapter 10 – Triumph for Restriction

A consensus existed after World War I that European immigration should be limited. Limitations could have been imposed in many ways. It could have been done by limiting the total number of immigrants admitted, by limiting the admission of unskilled workers or by strengthening literacy requirements (first done in the *Literacy Test Act)*. The formula adopted was consistent with the conclusions announced by the Dillingham Commission. The Commission had concluded that immigrants from northern and western Europe were genetically superior to those from southern and eastern Europe and that U.S. immigration policy should preserve their dominance.
(http://immigrationtounitedstates.org/588-immigration-act-of-1917.html)

In 1920, Senator William Dillingham introduced a bill based on a national origins formula. Introduced as the **Emergency Quota Act**, it was presented as necessary to preserve the very existence of the United States. He proposed that the bill limit immigration from each European nation annually to no more than 5% of its total population already existing in the U.S. according to the Census of 1910. While seeming equitable its intent was clear. The largest ethnic groups in the U.S. as of 1910 were of British, Irish and German extraction, and 5% of each of those groups entering each year would greatly exceed the numbers of immigrants from eastern or southern European nations.

The chairman of the House Committee on Immigration was Albert Johnson, a Republican congressman from the state of Washington. Johnson was initially in favor of ending all immigration to the U.S. Johnson became president of the Eugenics Research Association of America. His position was that "new immigrants" could not be assimilated. They would remain hyphenated Americans – "Polish-Americans," "Italian-Americans," and "Greek-Americans." He campaigned as being in favor of a law to save the country from an onslaught of criminals, paupers and the mentally ill. His advisor was Madison Grant, Secretary of the New York Zoological Society, a firm believer in Eugenics and author of the book *The Passing of the Great Race in America*. Research conducted by his House committee focused on residents in poor houses, mental institutions and hospitals in congested urban areas. Its conclusions supported Johnson's positions. Johnson reshaped Dillingham's bill and the **Emergency Quota Act of 1921** was also referred to as the **Johnson Emergency Quota Act**. The compromise bill that came to the floor

in each house provided restricted immigration from each European nation to 3% of the number of its people in the U.S. according to the census of 1910. No quota was cited for China or Japan. The passage of the bill followed a bitter debate.
(http://immigrationtounitedstates.org/589-immigration-act-of-1921.html)

Supporting restriction in the midst of the recession in 1920, Samuel Gompers, President of the AFL stated that "…with 2,000,000 idle and thousands of immigrants pouring into the country every day, the dangers ahead are so serious that even the enemies of labor are fearful…" To many it seemed ironic that Gompers, of Jewish extraction, having immigrated to the U.S. from England in 1863 and having been naturalized in 1872 should have supported this act. He was accused of hypocrisy. He was unapologetic.

The Immigration Committee of the American Defense Society warned, "…America with safety cannot continue to be an asylum to all peoples of the earth …those now coming in are…largely of races untrained by inheritance to appreciate the institutions, laws, customs and traditions of the United States…they multiply our problems…from their ranks come a large proportion of the radicals, the terrorists and a number of criminal cases." Senator Howell Heflin, Democrat from Alabama declared, "Bolshevism is in power in Russia and agents of Lenin and Trotsky are now either here or are trying to get in in order to preach this devilish work in the United States."

(https://en.wikipedia.org/wiki/American_Defense_Society)

Though in the minority, voices were raised in opposition to the bill. Congressman Adolph Sabath, representing an immigrant neighborhood in Chicago, led the opposition. He decried the idea that there was a national emergency. He cited the recent report of the Secretary of Labor which noted that in the fiscal year of 1919, 237,000 immigrants entered the U.S. in while 216,000 left.

Senator James Reed, Democratic Congressman of Missouri stated, "Exaggeration and excitement …has recently become violently epidemic…the country has been led by excited propagandists to believe that our country is about to be overwhelmed by a countless horde…there has been no stage in American history when that cry was not heard."

An appeal was made to President Harding to oppose the legislation by the Grand Order of B'rit Abraham, a Jewish fraternal organization that opposed the bill because of the bill's discriminatory nature. Jews were among the most adversely affected by the quota system. In 1790, there were about 3,000 Jews in the U.S., mostly Sephardic. By 1890 their numbers had risen to 300,000, most of whom were part of the larger German migration. Large scale immigration from the Russian Empire began after Russia's promulgation of its May Laws in 1881, which constricted the region where Jews could live. Limited economic opportunity, periodic bloody pogroms (such as that in Kishinev in 1903) and letters about freedom in America led to large scale Jewish immigration.

Following the dissolution of the multi-ethnic Austrian-Hungarian Empire at the end of World War I, without a country of their own, Jews were a minority in each new national state where ultranationalists resented their presence. Statistics collected after the census of 1790 identified Jews as a separate nationality, but **The Emergency Quota Act of 1921** did not. Quotas allocated to each of the eastern European states were small, and the opportunity for Jews to obtain visas to enter America became limited. The petition of the Jewish fraternal order asked President Harding to recall that immigrants "…helped to build America and now it is proposed to keep out those who are seeking freedom from persecution...."

(https://immigration.laws.com/emergency-quota-act)

President Warren G. Harding had campaigned in favor of restriction. He called a special session of Congress for the purpose of enacting the **Emergency Quota Act of 1921**. For the first time strict limits were placed on the admission of immigrants from Europe. Recognizing the importance of cheap agricultural labor for farmers, no restrictions were placed upon immigration from Mexico and Canada. No quota was set aside for China and Japan.

Chapter 11 – The National Origins System

The 1920's witnessed the passage of three major immigration laws, each of which was more restrictive than its predecessor. The **Emergency Quota Act of 1921** was the first to restrict European immigration. The formula adopted assigned numerical quotas per year to each nation based upon its number already settled in the U.S. in 1910. This was referred to as the *national origins system*. The **Immigration Acts of 1924 (Johnson-Reed Act)**, and the **National Origins Act of 1929** which followed, reduced established quotas even more. The primary targets for exclusion were Italians, Jews and Greeks.

(https://history.state.gov/milestones/1921-1936/immigration-act)

(http://archive.spectator.co.uk/article/15th-june-1929/8/the-united-states-national-origins-bill)

The quotas established by the **Emergency Quota Act of 1921,** when computed, limited total immigration to 357,000. When that number of admitted immigrants was reached, ships with immigrants were turned away. The number of slots allocated to applicants from northern and western Europe (Britain, Ireland and Germany) was approximately 175,000. A similar quota was made available to the nations of southern and eastern Europe. The numbers appeared equal but the impact of the law was not. The number of immigrants from northern and western Europe had not exceeded the 175,000 in the years just prior to the enactment of the law and its impact on that part of Europe was minimal. The number of immigrants from southern and eastern Europe had been 685,000 in each of the years just prior to the new law, and the impact on people hoping to immigrate to the U.S. from those nations was dramatic. This act was meant to regulate immigration for a single year but was extended for two additional years. (http://immigrationtounitedstates.org/589-immigration-act-of-1921.html)

The Emergency Quota Act of 1921 had an immediate impact in reducing immigration. In 1921, total immigration was 805,228; in 1922 the total fell to 309,556. Italian immigration was 222,269 in 1921, and fell to 40,319 in 1922. Eastern European immigration was 32,793 in 1921, and 12,224 in 1922. The national origins formula had sharply reduced the number of immigrants from southern and eastern Europe.

The **Immigration Act of 1924** (also called the **Johnson-Reed Act**) retained the national origins quota formula while adjusting its numbers. The number of immigrants to be admitted would be reduced from 3% to 2% of each nationality in the U.S. according to the Census in 1890. Rolling back the base from the census of 1910 to 1890, before the mass migration from southern and eastern Europe began, meant that fewer immigrants from those regions would be eligible to enter the United States. The projected quota for 1924-1925 for immigrants from Europe was 164,667. Preferences were given to relatives of residents under the age of 21, to parents, spouses and persons over 21 who were skilled in agriculture. As indicated in the chart below, immigration in 1925 (the year after the passage of the Act of 1924), overall immigration from all of eastern Europe fell to 1,566, and from Italy, fell to 6,203.

Year	Total Entering U.S.	Country of Origin		
		Great Britain	Eastern Europe*	Italy
1920	430,001	38,471	3,913	95,145
1921	805,228	51,142	32,793	222,260
1922	309,556	25,153	12,244	40,319
1923	522,919	45,759	16,082	46,674
1924	706,896	59,490	13,173	56,246
1925	294,314	27,172	1,566	6,203
1926	304,488	25,528	1,596	8,253

*Romania, Bulgaria and Turkey.
U.S. Bureau of the Census, *Historical Statistics of the United States, Colonial Times to 1957* (Washington, D.C., 1960), p. 56.

(https://www.u-s-history.com/pages/h1398.html)

The act also contained the **Asian Exclusion** provision which stated that "aliens by virtue of race or nationality ineligible for citizenship cannot be admitted." This provision barring all Asians was viewed as an act of humiliation in Japan. Foreign born wives and children of American citizens of Chinese extraction were denied admission.

New elements were added to the process of enforcing the new laws. Immigration policy would be made through cooperation between the State Department and Immigration and Naturalization Service. Officials in U.S. consulates appointed by the State Department would issue visas to persons they judged eligible for admission to the U.S. An applicant had to personally go to a U.S. consulate and apply for a visa. He would be interviewed regarding health, family, skills, personal beliefs and subjected to a medical examination. The person who satisfied all requirements would then be placed on a list to await a visa. An increasingly repeated criterion was used to determine eligibility whether an immigrant was "likely to become a public charge". Directives regarding the nature of vetting potential immigrants came to consuls from the State Department. The beliefs of state department officials became increasingly important in the directives consuls received. The consular system made the role of Ellis Island as an inspection center obsolete.

The Immigration Act of 1924 placed no restrictions on immigrants from any western hemisphere country. American farmers depended upon the labor from Mexico. Mexicans were free to immigrate to the U.S. and become naturalized citizens without any restriction. Although most Mexicans are a racial mix of Indian and European, for the purposes of immigration U.S. law considered them white. The border patrol, entrusted with the deportation of persons "excluded" by law who might cross the Mexican or Canadian borders was created in 1924.

The **National Origins Act of 1929** retained the quota system, but reduced the total number of immigrant admissions from 164,667 to 153,658. Eighty-five percent of those admitted would be from northern and western Europe. One of its most significant features was the reduction of the German quota from 51,227 to 24,908. It was upsetting to German Americans, but it would prove even more consequential for German Jews who would be looking for sanctuary after the Nazis came to power in 1933. By 1930 immigration from eastern and southern Europe came to nearly a complete halt.

Chapter 12 - The Immigration Crisis of 1939

The appointment of Adolph Hitler as Chancellor of Germany by President von Hindenburg in January 1933 was the first step in establishing a totalitarian Nazi state in Germany. That development produced one of the most agonizing immigration crises in history. It was not a crisis for the U.S., but rather for European Jews who found themselves in an expanding German Empire. For the U.S. it would pose the question of whether exceptions should be made to its restrictive immigration policy to provide a haven for endangered refugees. Some Americans believed that doing so was a moral imperative. Others did not.

Eugenics was at the center of Nazi ideology, its aim being the perfection of the Aryan (Germanic) race. In July 1933, the *Law for the Prevention of Hereditary Diseases* was enacted in Germany. The law required physicians to register every case of hereditary illness of their patients with Genetic Health Courts. In order to prevent reproduction among people with diseases deemed hereditary, 200 health courts ordered the sterilization of more than 400,000 people deemed epileptics, schizophrenics, manic-depressants, disabled by cerebral palsy, deaf or blind. The T4 program referred to as "endlosung," "mercy killing" took the lives of 70,000 before being discontinued in 1941. Thereafter it was transferred to concentration camps.

Nazi eugenic theorists formulated a hierarchy of races, with the Aryan (Nordic and Germanic) being at the top and products of the Anglo-Saxon invasions with Slavs falling low on the list. As they interpreted social Darwinism, superior races were destined to govern. In Nazi ideology Jews were not defined as Germans of the Jewish religious faith but as a race, a negative biological entity, the counterpoint to Germanic racial purity which had to be eliminated from the Germanic gene pool.

Out of 67 million Germans there were 535,000 Jews in Germany. Approximately 300,000 practiced forms of the Jewish religious faith. Approximately 125,000 had intermarried and identified as Lutherans while another 75,000 had done so with Catholics. Jews, as defined by blood (having one Jewish grandparent) made up (.07%), seven tenths of one percent of the German population. Twelve thousand German Jews died in defense of the "fatherland" during World War I. There is no single explanation of the Nazi obsession with the imperative to eliminate Jews from society.

Beginning in April 1933 with the boycott of Jewish businesses, laws were made to deny Jews the right to teach, practice law or hold government positions. Jews were expelled from the Culturbund, thus denying them access to the mass media or theatre. In 1935 the Nuremberg Laws revoked their citizenship and criminalized physical relationships between Jews and Aryans (term used to describe pure blooded, non-Jewish Germans). Approximately 170,000 Jews left Germany between January 1933 and November 1938.

In 1938 German forces marched into Austria. About 170,000 Jews were Austrians. All German laws meant to separate Jews from non-Jews were applied to Jews in Austria. A systematic process was introduced whereby Jews had to sign over all property in order to get an exit visa. Those unable to find refuge outside of Austria were threatened with imprisonment at the Mauthausen concentration camp. Sixty thousand Austrian Jews would die in Nazi death camps. William Shirer, then a reporter in Berlin, who wrote *The Rise and Fall of the Third Reich,* described the terror as Jews were beaten and forced to scrub the streets. The understaffed American consulate was deluged with people seeking refuge. Aware of what was taking place in Austria,

Monroe Deutch, vice-president and Provost of the University of California at Berkley wrote to President Franklyn D. Roosevelt asking that additional personnel be assigned to the consulate in Vienna. The response he received from M.H. McIntyre, Secretary to the president read,

> Much of the work requires special training and experience...You will understand that there are limits beyond which it is not practicable to go into detail...Because so many of these immigrants are required to leave Germany practically penniless and are dependent on relatives...for assistance and support...it has been found necessary to limit the validity of current affidavits of support and other assurances that the new refugees will not become a public charge to a period of one year ... names have been registered with incorrect spelling...Because there are now one hundred and thousand applications pending...it is not practical to give immediate consideration to all of these applications. (Zornberg, p.134-35)

President Roosevelt called an international conference to deal with the problem of resettling refugees from Germany. The nations of Latin America, France, Britain, Australia and Canada were represented. The Conference convened at Evian-les Baines in France on June 7, 1938. Representing the U.S. was Myron Taylor, former head of U.S. Steel and a friend of the president. He began by announcing that the U.S. was adding the

Austrian yearly quota to that of Germany (a total of approximately 27,000), but stated that no nation would be asked to modify its immigration laws.

Before the conference began, Britain announced it would not allow the subject of immigration to Palestine to be on the agenda. It was Britain that had been given a mandate by the League of Nations to govern Palestine (promising in its Balfour Declaration during World War I to create a Jewish national homeland in Palestine). The conference was a failure. With the exception of the Dominican Republic, which offered to receive 100,000 refugees, no other nation agreed to receive more than a few thousand refugees.

Two nations which were not invited sent representatives, Poland and Romania. They came to learn how they might reduce their Jewish populations. At the conclusion of the conference Poland announced that it was restricting the return of Polish citizens who had worked in Germany for many years. Its intent was to prevent the return of Jews. Reinhard Heydrich, head of the Gestapo ordered the round-up of thousands of Polish Jewish citizens and had them sent into a no-man's land between the borders of Germany and Poland. A letter by members of the Greenspan family to their son in Paris, describing the November cold to which the family was exposed, led the seventeen-year-old to go to the German embassy and shoot a consul whom he thought was the German ambassador. The death of Ernst von Rath became the Nazi justification for unleashing systematic terror by Nazi Party members on Jewish communities in Germany, Austria and Sudetenland on November 9th and 10th, 1938. The flames of burning synagogues made broken glass appear like crystal, and Krystallnacht is the generally recognized term for recalling what had taken place.

Previously anti-Semitic acts were directed by laws. On November 9th and 10th, 1938, Jews were denied the protection of the law. Firemen were told to protect only Aryan property while that of Jews would be allowed to burn. Two hundred and sixty-seven synagogues and Jewish communal buildings were burned. Seventy-five hundred Jewish shops were burned and looted. Homes were invaded and more than a hundred people were murdered. Thirty thousand Jewish men were arrested and sent to concentration camps. Jewish shop keepers were ordered to repair shops at their own expense (insurance claims going to the government) and the Jewish Community (Reichsvertretung der Deutches Juden) was fined one billion Reichsmarks for angering the German people. On November 12, 1938, it was ordered that all Jewish shops close by December 31, 1938, permanently. On November 15, 1938all Jewish children were expelled from German schools and on November 18, it was ordered that all Jews be excluded from the welfare system. Jewish institutional life was extinguished.

The British government at that moment was preparing a policy statement repudiating the Balfour Declaration; its new policy would strictly limit Jewish immigration to Palestine (White Paper, May 17, 1939). In England, there were people who acted to help German Jews. Laura Bracey, a Quaker working closely with Jewish, Protestant and Catholic immigrant assistance groups prevailed upon Prime Minister Chamberlain to allow the admission of "unaccompanied" German children to Britain. The Kindertransport, organized by Quakers and other good people, brought an estimated 10,000 unaccompanied children to Britain. People who volunteered to play a role in this effort met with parents willing to surrender the care of their children to strangers. Volunteers personally transported children out of Germany and delivered them to families in Britain who cared and provided for them.

In the United States, many people called upon President Roosevelt to act. On November 16, 1938, Senator James F. Byrnes of South Carolina wrote to the president:

> More expressions of our sympathy... offer no practical relief to the unfortunate Jews of Germany...I assume legislation is necessary to increase the quota of German citizens eligible for admission to this country...You could be assured of the cooperation of the Congress. Certainly, you will have my cooperation."

The president wrote back thanking him for his cooperation and added, "...we are working on the problem." (FDR Library)

On that same day, November 16, 1938, a letter was sent to the President by Congressman Charles A. Buckley of New York. It asked the president to support legislation that would admit refugees to the virtually empty territory of Alaska. The president responded,

> I have received your letter of November 16, 1938 concerning the possibility of settling refugees in Alaska and of offering in this connection to introduce a bill in Congress...excluding Alaska from the numerical limitations...of the existing immigration laws. I must state frankly...I do not favor legislation of the character you suggest...this would in effect make Alaska a foreign territory...which would obviously be out of the question. (FDR Library)

The crisis following the "Night of the Broken Glass" was not an American crisis, but a crisis facing European Jews. For the United States it was a question of deciding whether to open its gates and enable greater numbers of refugees to find sanctuary or to reject any such efforts.

Chapter 13 – Closing the Gates to Refugees

On November 14, 1938, on a nationwide radio program sponsored by the National Council of Churches, former President Herbert Hoover issued an appeal to the German people calling upon them to repudiate what had taken place on November 9 and 10, 1938. Former President Hoover was well suited to issue such an appeal.

Most historians praise F.D.R. for his New Deal policies during the Great Depression, and few have kind words for his predecessor. They fail to recognize an exceptional American. Hoover, a Quaker, was orphaned at a young age and went to live with an uncle, a doctor and Indian agent. Recognizing his own interest in math, Hoover registered to study engineering in Stanford University's opening class. Upon graduating, with his first job in a coal mine, he came to be recognized as a master engineer who developed production systems for mining in the U.S., Australia and China. At the start of World War I, Hoover and his wife were in London. Belgium was occupied by the Germans, blockaded by the British and faced starvation. After he successfully organized the evacuation of all Americans from war zones, the U.S.

Ambassador prevailed upon Hoover to feed the people of Belgium. From 1914 until the U.S. entered the War, he raised the funding to feed ten million people. When the U.S. entered the war, President Wilson asked him to supply American troops and allies with food. When the armistice ending the violence was signed in January 1918, he was placed in charge of the European Economic Council (supervising allied reconstruction). Aware of starvation in Germany, Hoover pressured Britain to lift its blockade and allow food into Germany. To feed German children he employed his own staff, and members of Quaker communities throughout Germany. Quakers fed a million children for more than a year; it was called Quakerspeisung. The favorable way in which the Quakers were remembered explains why they were able to assume leadership roles in the Kindertransport.

In his address to the German people, Hoover declared:

> Americans should and are expressing their indignation at the terrible Outbreak of persecution…This outrage does not represent the German People…. This comes squarely from the oppressors under whom the German people are living. Americans have more than usual right among the nations of the world to make this protest….It was Americans who insisted that German people should have food…the suffering being inflicted on an innocent and helpless people grieves every decent American.
> (http://hoover.archives.gov)

A Quaker mission, led by Rufus Jones, who had organized the American Friends Service Committee sailed for Germany shortly thereafter. It insisted upon and was given the right to assist the victims of violence. Letters from Hoover indicated his promise to provide monetary assistance. Jones' letters to Clarence Pickett, the executive director of the American Friends Service Committee informed him of the incarceration of Jewish men in concentration camps, the destruction of families and the destruction of all Jewish networks of self-help. Those letters encouraged Pickett to join together with other concerned Americans in an effort to replicate the Kindertransport in the United States.

Marion Kenworthy, a psychiatrist and psychoanalyst in New York specializing in children's mental health issues organized the Non-Sectarian Committee for German Refugee Children. A precise plan was formulated in which a Quaker network would vet children in Europe, transport them out of Germany and find homes for them in America. It would cost the government nothing. The plan required legislation to admit refugee children outside of the small German quota. The Wagner-Rogers bill, introduced in congress provided for the admission of twenty thousand "unaccompanied children" over a period of two years. Marion Kenworthy met with the

President's Advisory Committee on Refugees and explained the entire plan. It was hoped that the president would lend his support to the bill.

Clarence Pickett, who was a friend of the Roosevelts, agreed to serve as Executive Director of The Nonsectarian Committee. Pickett raised funds for a national lobbying effort and personally contacted witnesses who testified in Congress in support of the Wagner-Rogers Bill.

The Wagner-Rogers bill was introduced on February 13, 1939. Its two sponsors were Senator Robert Wagner of New York, a Catholic Democrat and Representative Edith Norse Rogers, a Protestant Republican from Massachusetts. A joint House- Senate Committee approved the bill. Upon its being returned to each house for consideration it met fierce opposition.

The fate of the Wagner-Rogers Bill was decided in the House. Testimony by advocates and opponents of the bill was offered over a three day period. Both the American Federation of Labor and Congress of Industrial Organization, which had supported increased restrictions on immigration in the past came out in support of the Wagner-Rogers Bill.   John Brophy, National Director of the C.I.O testified,

> I appear in support of House Joint Resolution 165,,, This statement is made in the name of the 4,000,000 men and women who make up the C.I.O. On February 9th the president of the C.I.O. John L. Lewis came out in full Support of this bill when he said, 'Assuredly America should do its part in caring for some of the children who are victims of religious and racial oppression in Germany.... There is something particularly revolting when it is practiced on little children. (Committee Hearings, pp. 91, 92)

Quentin Reynolds, noted journalist and writer for *Collier's Weekly* reported on his trip to Germany in December, 1938 to see what was taking place. He recounted,

> ...Jewish children are not allowed in the parks...In Berlin I stood in a ...line which at the end of November had been going on for two years...the 'hilfsverein' where the Jews were fed by their own people...After November 10 all private property was confiscated...and all of the various 'hilfsverein' stopped functioning. Their children can get no medical attention. Jewish doctors are not permitted to practice, and Aryan doctors cannot doctor them." (Committee Hearings, p. 83, 84)

In opposing the bill, James L. Wilmeth, National Secretary of the Junior Order United American Mechanics testified. The origin of this group can be traced back to its nativist and anti-catholic founders in the 1840s. Wilmeth stated:

> We have come in opposition to orphan children...we have plenty of that kind in America today... It is unnecessary to set aside or go beyond the fixed quotas ...We do not feel that suffering can be made the criterion...the persecution of people in Germany is limited to certain racial and religious minorities, and that the criterion is not one affecting the entire German people. We feel that the quota laws of 1924...are in need of revision...down rather than upward. (Committee Hearings, pp. 119,120)

Francis H. Kinnicutt, President of the Allied Patriotic Societies, Inc, New York City stated the objections of his organization to the bill,

1) On humanitarian grounds...children should not be separated from their parents and that foster parentage...is prejudicial to children

2) These children would soon compete with American children for jobs

3) The passage of the resolution...would lead to the further breakdown of Immigration quotas. (Committee Hearings, p. 136)

The bill which emerged from the House Committee on Immigration and Naturalization gave preference to "unaccompanied children" as part of the quota from

Germany but not in addition to it. Senator Wagner withdrew the bill from consideration. While Eleanor Roosevelt had publicly endorsed the bill, the president would not.

On May 13, 1939, the MS Saint Louis left Hamburg for Cuba with 908 Jewish refugees. All had legally purchased visas for admission to Cuba. In the two-week period before their arrival the Cuban government changed its policy. Twenty-two were allowed to disembark in Cuba. Captain Gustav Schroeder, the German captain empathized with his passengers. He set sail for Florida hoping that they would be admitted to the United States. Refugees could see the lights of Miami. There were many emotional appeals to President Roosevelt to admit the refugees, but the president was unmoved. Coast Guard cutters shadowed the ship to make certain that it would not be run aground. Passengers were denied permission to land as tourists since they were unable to provide a return address. Schroeder returned to Europe, but would not return to Germany until his passengers were accepted in a variety of European nations.

Chapter 14 – Impact of World War II

Many Americans believed that the U.S. should adhere to isolationism (avoid alliances) and adhere to neutrality (not taking sides); they spoke of the war in Europe as a struggle between Red and Black (Fascism and Communism) and felt that it was none of our business. The **Alien Registration Act**, also known as the **Smith Act** was enacted on January 29, 1940. It imposed criminal penalties on any persons advocating the violent overthrow of the government of the United States and required all aliens to register with the government. This would be done in local post-offices.

(http://tucnak.fsv.cuni.cz/~calda/Documents/1940s/Alien%20Registration%20Act%20of%201940.html)

The bombing of Pearl Harbor by the Empire of Japan on December 7, 1941 challenged American security. On December 11, 1941 both Nazi Germany and Fascist Italy, members of the Tripartite Agreement with Japan declared war upon the United States.

Internment

Attention focused upon Germans, Italians and Japanese, whose loyalty to the nation of their origin might make them a threat to American society. There were 695,000 Italians and 1.2 million Germans who had been born abroad and immigrated in the United States. In 1942, the FBI arrested 3,200 Italian resident aliens and 300 were interned. 11,000 German, including some naturalized citizens were arrested and 5,000 were interned.

Most affected by the bombing of Pearl Harbor were Japanese Americans, 75% of whom lived along the west coast. One account explains the fate of Japanese Americans in the following way, "On the west coast, long-standing racism against Japanese, motivated in part by jealousy over their commercial success, erupted after Pearl Harbor into furious demands to remove them en masse...Japanese immigrants and their descendants were rounded up and placed in detention centers...."
(https://www.history.com/this-day-in-history/fdr-signs-executive-order-9066)

Executive Order 9066, signed by President Roosevelt, gave the military power to take measures necessary for national security. *Civilian Exclusion Order14* promulgated by the commanding general, under the authority of Order 9066, ordered the exclusion of Japanese from the west military area by May 9 and removed to relocation centers. On March 18, 1942, the War Relocation Authority was established by a second Executive Order of the President. 127,000 Japanese were compelled to move to militarily controlled camps in the interior; 80,000 of those relocated were native born Americans.

On May 3. 1942, Fred Korematsu, who had been born in the U.S., refused to submit t relocation. He was convicted of violating a military order and sentenced to probation. He and his family were sent to the Topaz camp in Utah. His case was appealed to the Supreme Court of the U.S. The 6-3 ruling, issued on October 11, 1944 upheld his conviction. In the majority opinion, Justice Hugo Black wrote,

> Compulsory exclusion of large groups of people from their homes, except under conditions of direst emergency and peril is inconsistent with our basic governmental institutions. But when, under conditions of modern warfare our shores are threatened by hostile forces, the power to protect must be commensurate with the threatened danger.

In his dissent, Justice Murphy wrote: "I dissent, therefore, from the legalization of racism. Racial discrimination in any form and any degree has no justification in our democratic way of life."
(https://en.wikipedia.org/wiki/Korematsu_v._United_Sta tes)

It wasn't until during the presidency of Ronald Reagan, that Congress enacted the Civil Liberties Act of 1988.

The act contained an apology and provided reparation payments to surviving internees.
([https://www.npr.org/sections/codeswitch/2013/08/09/21](https://www.npr.org/sections/codeswitch/2013/08/09/210138278/japanese-internment-redress) 0138278/japanese-internment-redress)

Assuring a Supply of Labor

In August 1942, the United States and Mexico signed the **Bracero Agreement.** It was an agreement between two governments to supply additional labor to America. Under the Agreement, the "employer" responsible for implementing the terms of the agreement was the Farm Security Administration of the U.S. Department of Agriculture. The word *bracero* translates as *one with strong hands*. Farmers to whom "labor" would be provided would be called "sub-employers." Under the Agreement the employer would be responsible for all transportation and repatriation costs, would assure payment of $3.00 a day for living expenses and a minimum hourly wage of .30 per hour for Mexican laborers. The U.S. government was charged with making certain that there would be no discrimination (Executive Order 8802) against any Mexican worker. Workers would elect their own representatives to interact with their employer. An important provision relating to immigration stated that any worker remaining in the U.S. upon completion of his contract would be considered illegal. This agreement, negotiated in 1942 would remain in effect until 1964. It is estimated that 4.5 million Mexican workers came to the U.S. as part of that agreement.

(http://farmworkers.org/bpaccord.html)

Re-evaluating the status of a Chinese Ally

With China considered an ally in the war against Japan, on December 17, 1943 Congress enacted and the President signed the **Magnuson Act** into law. The act also known as an **Act to Repeal the Chinese Exclusion Act**, repealed all accumulated acts that had focused on Chinese exclusion, allowed Chinese residents to be naturalized, and allocated a quota for Chinese immigration under the Immigration Act of 1924. Given the 2% for each nationality in the U.S. in 1890, the quota allowed 105 immigrants to enter the U.S. from China each year.

(https://history.state.gov/milestones/1937-1945/chinese-exclusion-act-repeal)

An Act to Save Lives of remaining European Jews

In January 1944, Randolph Paul delivered a report to Secretary of the Treasure Henry Morgenthau entitled *Report to the Secretary on the Acquiescence of this government to the murder of the Jews."* The report documented State Department procrastination in delivering funds that could have assisted refugee escape,

and accused the State Department of concealing reports of the mass murder of Jews. Three days later Morgenthau, John Pehle and Randolph Paul met with the president who agreed to issue an executive order creating the War Refugee Board (WRB). The War Refugee Board's actions were subject to agreement between the Secretaries of State, Defense and Treasury. It was charged "with taking all measures to rescue those victims of enemy oppression who are in imminent danger of death." Up to this moment, saving Jews had not been a national priority.
(https://www.jewishvirtuallibrary.org/report-on-the-acquiescence-of-fdr-government-in-the-murder-of-the-jews-january-1944)

The WRB directed its efforts to saving members of the Hungarian Jewish community, the only significant Jewish community remaining in Nazi occupied Europe. Out of 800,000 Hungarian Jews, 400,000 had already been deported and sent to Auschwitz. Upon its appeal for assistance to the Swedish government (which was neutral in the war), Swedish businessman Raul Wallenberg was sent to Budapest. Wallenberg established safe houses for thousands of Jews in Budapest, and provided papers assuring Swedish protection to others. Wallenberg extracted people from the Nazi death march to Poland. Ira Hirshmann, WRB representative in Turkey gained support from Archbishop Angelo Roncalli who sent thousands of baptismal certificates to the papal nuncio in Hungary in an effort to save Jewish lives. Cardinal Roncalli would become Pope John XXIII. It is estimated that WRB efforts saved the lives of 200,000 people.

The War Refugee Board also established free ports in which refugees might find a haven until the end of the war. One free port was established in Oswego, New York. In *Operation Safe Haven*, 982 refugees were brought to the U.S. on a troop transport from Italy in July 1944. Five hundred and twenty-five were men and four hundred and fifty-seven were women, eight hundred and seventy-four were Jewish. Refugees were not given visas or resident status. They were viewed as part of a cargo in transit to be transshipped to the nations in which they lived at the war's end. Oswego was a camp with barbed wire fences, bright lights and military personnel. It was established by the War Relocation Authority which established detention camps for Japanese Americans. During the first two months its residents could not leave the camp and thereafter could walk only to town. Family members visited and town residents were remembered for their great kindness by the refugees. The camp was closed in June 1945. President

Truman allowed the refugees to stay. "To make it official, refugees were bused across the Rainbow Bridge to Niagara Falls, Canada, where immigration officers presented them with the necessary papers admitting them to the United States."

(https://www.oswego.edu/library/safe-haven)

Chapter 15 – The Truman Years

The death of President Roosevelt on April 12, 1945 brought Harry S. Truman to the helm one month before the unconditional surrender of Nazi Germany (May 8, 1945). Never having been informed by his predecessor of the development of the atomic bomb, Truman would be compelled to make world changing decisions. In response to Soviet expansionism in Europe, Truman developed the important policy of containment.

One of the more pleasant pieces of legislation the new president signed into law in 1945 was the **War Brides Act.** The act provided for the admission of fiancés (women to be married within three months) wives and children of American servicemen. Race was not to be a determining factor. Among wives and children were Chinese, Japanese and Filipino women. Under this act, 127,000 brides and 25,000 children immigrated to the United States.
(https://warbridesof1945.weebly.com/war-brides-act.html)

Truman believed it important to help address the refugee crisis in Europe. His attention increasingly focused on assisting people in Displaced Persons Camps (DP Camps) established in the American Zone of

Occupation. Camps were envisioned as temporary locations from which persons liberated or on the move would return to their former homes. For those certain that their towns and homes no longer existed the camps assumed a more permanent presence.

As World War II came to an end millions of people were on the move. Prisoners of war, forced laborers brought to Germany from Nazi occupied countries, and people liberated from Nazi concentration camps were free to return to their homes. As Soviet armies advanced west, thousands fearing Soviet retribution fled before them. When the Nazis occupied the Baltic States (Latvia, Lithuanian and Estonia) they found supporters who were both anti-Russian and anti-Semitic and who joined the Waffen SS. The Nazis had also organized an army of Ukrainians to fight the Soviet Union. Many of these people, fearing Soviet retribution, fled west.

Volksdeutche, considered Germans by race by the Nazi government, lived in many Eastern European nations. They were encouraged to organize and support Nazi objectives. Unrest in the Sudetenland in 1935, then part of Czechoslovakia, resulted in the dismemberment of Czechoslovakia. Before the start of World War II, the German American Bund operated Nazi training camps in

New York and New Jersey. In Poland, during the war the Selbschutz (organized units of ethnic Germans) played a role in "eliminating" the Polish intelligentsia and benefitted from the confiscation of Jewish property. In Hungary 54,000 joined the SS. At the war's end in 1945, volksdeutche who joined the Nazis as well as innocent Germans who did not were driven out of many of the regions in which they had previously lived. An estimated 12 million people were on the move as the war came to an end. At one point, 850,000 people found shelter in Displaced Persons camps.

Among the millions on the move were nearly half a million Jewish survivors of the Nazi genocide. With the liberation of the death camps, assistance was provided by liberating forces and religious relief agencies. Many near death were slowly fed and rehabilitated while others were too weak to survive. Whereas the allied objective was to resettle those liberated to their own native countries, Jews often found hostility when they sought out surviving relatives in native towns which had previously been their homes. Non-Jews who had been given the homes and possessions of Jews removed by the Nazis now feared their return. One of the most violent attacks on returning Jews took place in Kielce, Poland on July 1, 1946. Before the war 24,000 Jews lived in Kielce, approximately one third of its population. 200 returned after 1945. A non-Jewish Polish boy who had stayed away from home told of his having been abducted by Jews. Recalling the "blood libel," the tale told by anti-Semites, that Jews needed the blood of Christian children for their religious rituals, hundreds attacked the Jewish center, including police officers, murdered 45 Jews and wounded 40 others. The Polish government tried and executed nine killers. About 75,000 Jews, most of whom had returned to Poland from Russia, headed west. In Displaced Persons Camps, they found themselves sharing space with many anti-Semites who had formerly cooperated with the Nazis in murdering Jews.

In a number of memoranda, President Truman appealed to Congress to address the subject, and in some instances issued executive decrees when Congress failed to act. On December 22, 1945, he issued an order to the military. It read,

> Every effort is being made to return displaced persons to their homes…The great difficulty is that so many of these persons have no homes to which they may return… To the extent that our immigration laws permit, everything possible should be done at once to facilitate the entrance of some of these displaced persons and refugees to the United States. I consider that common

decency...requires us to do what lies within our power. The period of unacceptable distress is not the time for us to close or narrow our gates. (https://www.trumanlibrary.org/educ/dps/Truman Directive.pdf)

A second memorandum on that same date directed a number of specific steps be taken. The Attorney General was directed to appoint vice consuls who could issue visas. Reasoning that the Consular system was no longer operable, the directive took the power of vetting out of the hands of the State Department. The Secretary of War was directed to feed, house and provide medical care in DP camps under U.S. control and to make transportation available to bring immigrants to European ports. The Attorney General was directed to assign personal to Oswego, to determine how many persons had been on lists applying for immigration before the war began and to facilitate the admission of persons eligible. Truman ordered the creation of an independent commission under the Commissioner of Immigration and Naturalization to investigate conditions in the camps. It was at their direction that Jews in DP camps were allowed to organize independently and live apart from those who fled the Soviets. Truman also pressured the British to allow 100,000 Jewish refugees into Palestine.

Little action was taken in Congress until the passage of the **Displaced Person's Act** in 1948. In the Senate, Republican Senator Chapman Rivercomb of West Virginia chaired the Immigration Subcommittee of the Senate Judiciary Committee. Rivercomb was one of seven senators who voted against the U.S. joining the United Nations. In December 1946, in referring to DP's, he declared, "…it would be a tragic blunder to bring into our midst those imbued with communist lines of thought when one of the most important tasks is to combat and eradicate communism from this country." As the process advanced, he insisted that a committee visit DP camps in Europe. The committee headed by Paul Griffin, Commander of the American Legion surprised Rivercombe when he returned with a call for immediate action. Senator William Langer of North Dakota insisted that preference be given to admit Volksdeutche. He stated that the Volksdeutche were much worse off than "the so-called displaced persons…related to residents (i.e. Jews) in New York City."
(http://www.yadvashem.org/odot_pdf/Microsoft Word - 3541.pdf)

The Displaced Person's Act of 1948 provided for the admission of 200,000 immigrants over a period of two years. Eligibility was restricted to persons in camps in Germany, Austria and Italy on or before December 27,

1945. Numbers admitted from each nation would be deducted from future quota admissions. An amendment gave preference to volksdeutche and to persons with agricultural skills. Since Nazi Germany surrendered in May 1945, it was not possible for many Jews to have been in allied camps by December 27, 1945; in effect, the Displaced Persons Act of 1948 excluded almost all Jews from inclusion among the 200,000 potential immigrants.

(http://immigrationtounitedstates.org/464-displaced-persons-act-of-1948.html)

In signing the bill, President Truman declared,

> It is with very great reluctance that I have signed... the **Displaced Persons Act of 1948**. ...In its present form it is flagrantly discriminatory. It mocks the American tradition of fair play... I have decided ... that it would not be right to penalize the beneficiaries of this bill on account of the injustices perpetrated against others... the bill discriminates in callous fashion against displaced persons of the Jewish faith. The primary device...is the provision restricting eligibility to those displaced persons who entered Germany, Austria or Italy on or before Decmeber 27, 1945. Most of the Jewish displaced persons...arrived after December 27, 1945. It is inexplicable except upon the abhorrent ground of intolerance. The date Should have been April 21, 1947, the day on which the displacement camps were closed to further admissions.
> (http://www.presidency.ucsb.edu/ws/index.php?pid=12942)

Truman appointed commissioners Ugo Cotrusi, Edward M. O'Connor and Henry N. Rosenthal to enforce the law. To the dismay of some congressmen, they interpreted the law in a way that permitted the immigration of a greater numbers of Jewish displaced persons. In 1950 there was a follow-up to the **Displaced Persons Act of 1948** which permitted persons who entered the camps as late as 1949 to claim DP status.

By 1952, 400,000 refugees had been admitted to the U.S. including 63,000 Jews. Most Jewish refugees immigrated to the State of Israel after its establishment in 1948.

By 1952, with the start of the Cold War, the nature of the debate over immigration shifted from concern for refugees to national security. One of the most moving bronze freezes in the World War II Memorial in Washington, D.C. depicts an American and Russian soldier hugging each other when they met at the Elba River. Not long after the end of World War II, the U.S. confronted an expansive Soviet Union which imposed its military and political control over most of the nations of central and Eastern Europe. The Soviets claimed the ideological superiority of Communism over Capitalism, and the "dictatorship of the proletariat" over democracy. Congressmen added persons with those beliefs to categories of "undesirable qualities," justifying their exclusion.

The Immigration and Nationality Act of 1952 also known as the **McCarran-Walter Act** was a response to the Cold War. It was sponsored by two Democrats, Paul McCarran of Nevada and Frances Walter of Pennsylvania. While maintaining the quota system introduced in the Immigration Acts of 1924 and 1929, it set the number of persons to be admitted each year to 270,000. Family members and individuals with special skills were exempt from quotas. An important element was its elimination of the racial barriers to naturalization imposed in the Immigration Act of 1790. This law, for which Chinese, Japanese, Filipino and Korean organizations lobbied, allowed for naturalization of immigrants from China and Japan. Each nation was awarded a small immigration quota. The act permitted the admission of 2,000 immigrants from the "Asia barred" zone.
(https://history.state.gov/milestones/1945-1952/immigration-act)

The primary focus of this bill was on the exclusion of persons deemed subversive. The Immigration Act of

1906 excluded anarchists. The Immigration Act of 1952 excluded communists, members of communist front organizations, and persons deemed subversive by the Attorney General of the United States. It empowered the Justice Department to deport immigrants or naturalized citizens engaged in subversive activities. Also excluded were people who believed in or practiced polygamy, drunkards, and adulterers. Despite the bill's sponsorship by members of his own party President Truman vetoed the bill. He objected to its retention of the national origins system. His veto was overridden and the bill became a law on June 27, 1952. Critics of the bill noted that among those denied admission by the Justice Department because of their leftist leanings were Chilean Poet and Nobel Prize Winner Pablo Neruda, Colombian writer and Nobel Prize winner Gabriel Garcia Marquez and Pierre Trudeau before he became prime minister of Canada.

A subject given greater attention was a dramatic increase in the number of people from Mexico who were illegally in the U.S. By illegal, we mean people who were in the U.S. without having received consular approval or contracts under the Bracero Agreement. Truman recognized the value of the Bracero Agreement to American farmers. He was intent on the enforcement of

a provision in the agreement which required laborers to return home at the end of their contracts. In 1950 a Presidential Commission on Migratory Labor was established. It blamed employers who would pay illegals lower wages than was agreed upon in the Bracero Agreement for encouraging illegal immigration. Congress rejected the president's request that employers of illegal workers be fined. Statistics indicate 127,000 deportations during the Truman years while 3.2 million left voluntarily rather than face deportation.
(https://www.factcheck.org/2010/07/hoover-truman-ike-mass-deporters/).

Dwight Eisenhower became president in January 1953 and took dramatic steps to drive illegals from the south and southwest. His action, termed Operation Wetback, coordinated with the government of Mexico, resembled a military operation. More than 1,000 border agents divided into teams raided neighborhoods known to house illegal workers. Each team was provided with busses, ships and aircraft. Illegal workers were loaded onto them and deported to Mexico. Those who returned were deposited deep inside Mexico. During the first month 50,000 were deported and 500,000 fled to avoid arrest. Ships unloaded deportees in Vera Cruz. During the operation which lasted three months, an estimated 1.3 million people left the United States for Mexico.

One result of the operation was the common use of the term "wetback" by bigots to describe Mexicans here under the Bracero Agreement (445,000 in 1956) and U.S. citizens of Mexican origin.

(https://thefederalistpapers.org/us/how-eisenhower-dealt-with-Americas-first-illegal-crisis)

Chapter 16 – The Great Shift

At times a multiplicity of events, planned and unplanned, operating in serendipity can change both thought and action. In previous chapter 9, *"A Perfect Storm"* one becomes aware of developments which led to the most restrictive immigration policies in the history of our nation. The **Immigration Act of 1965** also known has the **Hart-Celler Act** passed the House with a vote of 320 in favor and 70 opposed. In the Senate 76 voted in favor and 18 were opposed. President Lyndon B. Johnson signed the **Immigration Act of 1965** into Law, on October 3, 1965. The Immigration Act of 1965 ended to the national origins formula which had determined the nature of U.S. immigration policies since 1921.

In signing the bill into law, on October 3, 1965, President Johnson declared, that "...the old system violated the basic principles of American democracy, the principle that values and rewards each man on the basis of his merits as a man. It has been un-American in the highest sense because it has been untrue to the faith that brought thousands to these shores even before we were a country." One is moved to ask, what had changed? (https://cis.org/Report/HartCeller-Immigration-Act-1965)

Both foreign and domestic considerations led to the passage of the Immigration Act of 1965. The U.S. no longer adhered to a policy of isolationism in the post-World War II period. The United States was a founder of the United Nations and a signer of the *Universal Declaration of Human Rights* (recognized the fundamental equality of human beings) and the *Genocide Convention.* We were involved in the Vietnam War and bound to allies in Asia. In Europe, we were critical of the denial of human rights in nations oppressed by the Soviet Union. It no longer seemed fitting to maintain a policy which assumed the superiority of some ethnic groups and the inferiority of others.

Domestic considerations also influenced American thinking. Americans in Europe had liberated Nazi death camps and were witnesses to a system driven by a racist ideology. After their sacrifices in the war and with our own nation's propaganda, African Americans and their supporters were emboldened to begin a struggle for full civil rights. The Supreme Court decision in Brown v Board of Education in 1954, declared "separate but equal in education" to be unequal. The defiance of Rosa Parks and Dr. King's speech during the March on Washington in 1962 took issue with racial discrimination.

(https://www.ohchr.org/EN/UDHR/Documents/UDHR_ Translations/eng.pdf)

Among the most important reasons for the Immigration Act of 1965 were the beliefs and convictions of two American presidents, John F. Kennedy and Lyndon B. Johnson. When he was seeking to establish his credentials in 1958, John F. Kennedy published the little-known book *A Nation of Immigrants*. His recall of the treatment of Irish immigrants was a factor in his denunciation of the national origins system. In a caustic remark Kennedy had once proposed changing some words in the poem *New Colossus* by Emma Lazarus (found that the base of the Statue of Liberty) from "Give me your tired and poor" to "give me your tired and poor as long as they come from northern Europe and are not too tired or too poor…(and) never stole a bread."

(https://www.goodreads.com/work/quotes/1423547-a-nation-of-immigrants)

Kennedy proposed family unification, skills necessary in the U.S. and then a "first come first serve" application process in a revised immigration law. His book was published by the Anti-Defamation League of B'nai Brit, a Jewish organization which recalled the rejection of a bill that would have allowed the admission of 20,000 unaccompanied children from Germany in 1939.

Following the assassination of John F. Kennedy on November 22, 1963, Lyndon B. Johnson became president of the U.S. Johnson, a Democrat who served in Congress from 1933 until he ran as Kennedy's vice-presidential running mate in 1960, was exceptional in many ways. Unfairly confined to back pages in history by many historians because of his support for the Vietnam War, he was responsible for the passage the Medicare and Medicaid bills and the Civil Rights Act of 1964 which dramatically changed American society. Making the refusal of any business in interstate commerce to serve African Americans a federal crime dealt a blow to racial segregation. Less well known of were his actions, legal and outside of the law, providing visas to small numbers of Jewish refugees in 1938 and 1939 and smuggling them into the port of Galveston. (http://lyndonjohnsonandisrael.blogspot.com/)

The Immigration Act of 1965 replaced the national origins system with a preference system. Two points in the act accentuate its difference. It pointedly states that the word "quota" should be replaced by the word "numbers." In describing availability of visas it states,

"No person shall receive any preference or priority or be discriminated against...because of race, sex, nationality, place of birth or place of residence...." (Public Law 89-236). The act then enumerated preferences consuls would be directed to consider in granting visas to immigrants.

The first priority was "family reunification," and 74% of visas were set aside for that purpose. The act stated that preference would be given to "...immediate relatives...who are otherwise qualified for admission...without regard to the numerical limitations of this Act." Family members identified were wives, parents and children of a citizen of the United States, married and unmarried sons and daughters (10% of visas), brothers and sisters (24%). The law stated that the number of permanent and conditional visas not exceed a total of 170,000 each year. Exempting family members from inclusion in the count led to a dramatic increase in immigration through what is now called "chain migration."

Ten percent of immigration visas were set aside for professionals (architects, lawyers, physicians, engineers and teachers) "who because of their exceptional ability in the sciences and the arts...substantially benefit...the national economy, cultural interests or welfare of the United States." Ten percent were set aside for workers in short supply and to persons who had assisted members of the American Foreign Service in their native countries. (Public Law-89-236-October 3, 1965). An estimated 6% was set aside for refugees.

(https://www.gpo.gov/fdsys/pkg/STATUTE-79/pdf/STATUTE-79-Pg911.pdf)

The Attorney General was empowered to admit individuals "…because of persecution or fear of persecution on account of race, religion or political opinion." Specifically noted was preference to applicants from the Middle East "unable or unwilling to return" to a country in which they might be persecuted. Visas for other immigrants would be subject to review by the Department of Labor which would determine whether the skills of an applicant were in demand in the U.S. or would negatively affect the wages of American workers. Such determinations would be sent to the State Department for transmission to consuls. Three departments reviewed petitions for a visa – the departments of Justice, Labor and State.

At a ceremony celebrating the signing of the bill, President Lyndon B. Johnson declared, "The bill we sign today is not a revolutionary bill. It does not affect the lives of millions." Senator Ted Kennedy of Massachusetts said, "It will not upset the ethnic balance of our society." Both President Johnson and Senator Kennedy were wrong. The bill set aside 170,000 visas a year for new immigrants but excluded "family reunification" and "special refugee status" from inclusion in that number. The bill expanded the definition of a family to include not only members of a citizen's nuclear family but also to his brothers, sisters and their children. What is now referred to as "chain migration" would greatly increase immigration. The graph below indicates the dramatic increase in immigration after 1965.

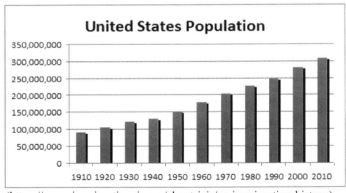

United States Population

(https://www.immigrationeis.org/about-ieis/us-immigration-history)

The ethnic balance Kennedy had in mind would change dramatically. In 1965, 84% of all Americans were of

European descent. Fewer than 5% were Hispanic, and fewer than 1% were Asians. Only 9.6% were foreign born. Between 1965 and 2015, 45 million people immigrated to the United States. 47% of those who entered legally were from Latin America (23% from Mexico) and 32.5% came from Asia. 14% of the U.S. population today is of Hispanic origin.
(https://search.uscis.gov/search?utf8=%E2%9C%93&aff iliate=uscis_gov&query=Annual+Report-on-the-impact-of-the-homeland)

The graph produced by the Pew Foundation, referring to immigration patterns between 1965 and 2015 as the **Modern Wave,** makes clear the changing ethnicity of immigrants between 1965 and 2015. According to those statistics 74% of immigrants came from Latin America or Asia.

FIGURE 1.1

Latin American, Asian Immigrants Make Up Most of Post-1965 Immigration

%

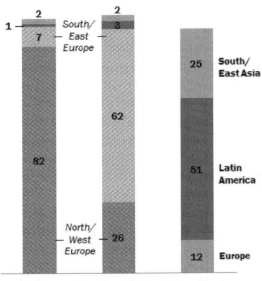

Northern
Europe Wave
(1840-1889)
14.3 million

Southern/Eastern
Europe Wave
(1890-1919)
18.2 million

Modern Wave
(1965-2015)
58.5 million

Note: Data for 1965–2015 include legal and unauthorized immigrants; for 1840–1919, only legal admissions.

Source: For 1965-2015, Pew Research Center estimates based on adjusted census data; for 1840-1919, Office of Immigration Statistics, Yearbook of Immigration Statistics, 2008, Table 2

PEW RESEARCH CENTER

(http://www.pewhispanic.org/2015/09/28/chapter-1-the-nations-immigration-laws-1920-to-today/)

Chapter 17 – Clusters of New Immigrants

Region and Country	Number of Immigrants	Percent (%)
Asia Total	12,750,000	100.0
Eastern Asia	3,951,000	31.0
China, excluding Taiwan	2,148,000	16.8
Taiwan	365,000	2.9
Japan	336,000	2.6
Korea, including South Korea and North Korea	1,080,000	8.5
South Central Asia	3,531,000	27.7
Bangladesh	210,000	1.6
India	2,206,000	17.3
Iran	365,000	2.9
Nepal	110,000	0.9
Pakistan	371,000	2.9
South Eastern Asia	4,153,000	32.6
Myanmar	128,000	1.0
Cambodia	163,000	1.3
Laos	194,000	1.5
Philippines	1,926,000	15.1
Thailand	252,000	2.0
Vietnam	1,292,000	10.1
Western Asia	1,062,000	8.3
Iraq	217,000	1.7
Israel	133,000	1.0
Lebanon	119,000	0.9
Other Asia	54,000	0.4

(https://www.migrationpolicy.org/article/asian-immigrants-united-states)

Statistics organized by the Migration Policy Institute, an immigration think tank in Washington D.C. indicate that 10,590,000 Asian immigrants from many different countries entered the U.S. between 1965 and 2014. The following chart offers a breakdown of the numbers of immigrants from each Asian nation and the percentage of the 10,590,000 from each nation.

Graphs charting the immigration patterns of Chinese and Filipino Immigrants, produced by the U.S. Census Bureau indicate the upward spiral of immigration from those nations.

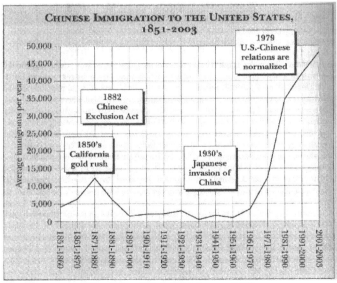

(Bankston III & Hidalgo, p.148)

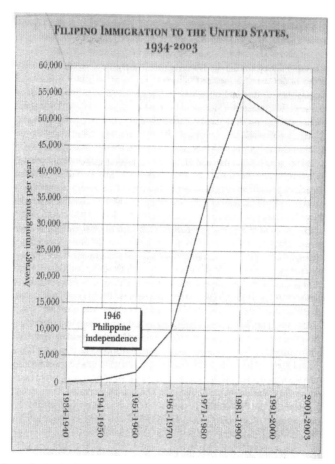

FILIPINO IMMIGRATION TO THE UNITED STATES, 1934-2003

(https://upload.wikimedia.org/wikipedia/commons/2/2a/Graph_of_Filipino_I
mmigrants_who_were_granted_LPR_Status_from_1930-2010.jpg)

A second region from which large numbers came after 1965 was the Caribbean. Four million people immigrated from Caribbean nations. The chart on the following page indicates their numbers and the percent of the estimated four million from each nation.

Region and Country	Number of Immigrants	Percent (%)
Caribbean	4,000,000	100.0
Cuba	1,173,000	29.3
Dominican Republic	998,000	24.9
Jamaica	706,000	17.6
Haiti	628,000	15.7
Trinidad and Tobago	220,000	5.5
Barbados	51,000	1.3
Grenada	34,000	0.9
Bahamas	32,000	0.8
Dominica	28,000	0.7
West Indies	26,000	0.6
St. Vincent and the Grenadines	23,000	0.6
Other Caribbean	81,000	2.0

(https://www.migrationpolicy.org/article/caribbean-immigrants-united-states)\

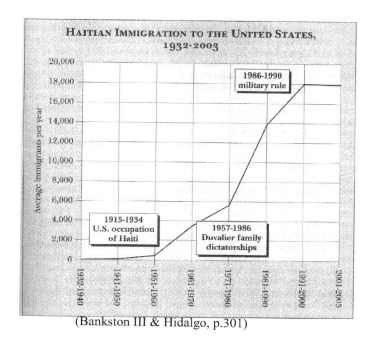

(Bankston III & Hidalgo, p.301)

Identifying the nations from which immigrants have come requires the study of geography.

Chapter 18 – "Special Cases"

Cubans

In 1958 Fidel Castro successfully led a revolution in Cuba which overthrew the dictatorship of Fulgencio Batista. Many Americans were initially sympathetic. Castro proceeded to imprison large numbers of Cubans and to establish a single party, Communist dictatorship. An estimated 79,000 Cubans immigrated to the U.S. by 1960. Others continued to flee from the Island. In 1966, Congress passed the **Cuban Adjustment Act.** It provided that Cuban citizens in the U.S. since January 1959, having been inspected and paroled, living in the U.S. for two years could apply and be granted permanent residency (a green card) by the Attorney General. By 1970 the number of Cubans reached 439,000. In 1980 the Cuban government 'turned a blind eye' to what came to be called the Mariel Boatlift. One-Hundred Twenty-Four Thousand (124,000) Cubans left Cuba by boat. Out of spite the Castro regime included "criminals" and "mentally ill" among those allowed to exit. In 1995 in an agreement with Cuba, a policy called the "wet foot, dry foot" was adopted. Cubans picked up at sea would be returned to Cuba while those who set foot on U.S. shores would remain.

On January 20, 2015, President Obama restored formal diplomatic relations with Communist Cuba. Applicants for immigration must now satisfy requirements established in the Immigration and Naturalization Act of 1965.

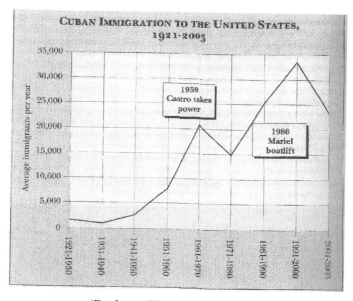

(Bankston III & Hidalgo, p.178)

Vietnamese

Before World War II Vietnam had been a French colony. During the War, Vietnam was occupied by Japan. French efforts to regain control after the war failed; the agreement ending French occupation provided that the north (Communist dominated) and south would be temporarily divided. Determined to unite Vietnam under its leadership, the government in the north under Ho Chi Minh invaded the south. Believing in the "domino theory" at that time, that communism would spread from one country to another, the U.S. assisted the government in the south and became deeply involved in the Vietnam War.

In 1973, after ten years of involvement, our government under President Nixon negotiated an exit from Vietnam. In May 1975, President Ford signed the **Indochina Migration and Refugee Act** into law. After the fall of Saigon (capital of South Vietnam) the U.S. evacuated approximately 100,000 Vietnamese to the U.S. One hundred twenty-five thousand others escaped to the Philippines and Guam, and most were admitted to the U.S. Between 1978 and 1980 large numbers of people, referred to as "boat people" took to the sea looking for sanctuary. Refugees from Cambodia, Laos and Vietnam were admitted as "special refugees." Congress appropriated more than $300 million to resettle these immigrants throughout the United States. Catholic, Protestant and Jewish organizations assisted in their resettlement. They were paroled and made eligible for permanent resident status. Chain migration permitted the addition of others. With a population of 1,292,000 in 2014, Vietnamese are the sixth largest immigrant group.

Some conservatives argued that these groups would be difficult to assimilate and objected to immigrants changing the demographic make-up of American society. Noted African American leader John Conyers, Congressman from Michigan, reacting to the fact that hundreds of millions of dollars were allocated for settling Indo Chinese refugees asked, "Should we be spending (federal dollars) on Vietnamese or should we spend them on Detroit refugees?"

(https://www.quora.com/Why-were-the-South-Vietnamese-allowed-to-enter-the-US-after-the-Vietnam-War)

The **Refugee Immigration Act of 1980** was passed by Congress on March 17, 1980. Its object was to establish procedures for admitting refugees. Without naming specific groups it stated, "If the president determines…an unforeseen refugee emergency exists…the president may fix the number of refugees to be admitted." It empowered the Attorney General to "admit any person who is outside any country of one's nationality, unable or unwilling to return" where persecution is "well founded: because of race, religion, nationality or political opinion." The Attorney General, after granting asylum could also adjust the status of the refugee and grant permanent residency. The act provided for the appointment of a U.S. Coordinator of Refugee

Affairs (with the title of an ambassador) subject to approval by the Senate, who would work out of the Department for Health and Human Services.

(Public Law 9=212)
https://www.congress.gov/111/plaws/publ212/PLAW-111publ212.pdf)

A program which few seem to remember in today's debate over the well-being of unaccompanied, undocumented children, is the **Unaccompanied Refugee Minor's Program** begun in 1980 during the presidency of James Earl Carter. This program was meant to facilitate the granting of visas to children born out of relations between male American soldiers and women in Vietnam and other nations in Southeast Asia. Federal money was provided to state coordinators who would see that children would be placed in safe homes. Children were generally not available for adoption. Faith-based organizations usually became overseers of proper child placement and care in these cases.
(https://www.acf.hhs.gov/orr/programs/urm/about)

The **Immigration Reform Bill of 1986**, known as the **Simpson-Mazzoli Bill,** addressed the subject of illegal immigration. It was also called the **Reagan Amnesty Bill**. Signed into law by President Ronald Reagan on November 6, 1986, the law legalized undocumented immigrants who entered the U.S. before January 1, 1982. The president believed that this act would clear the playing field and that the essence of the law would discourage future illegal immigration. Recognizing that employers encouraged illegal immigration, this law imposed sanctions on employers. It stated that an employer with three or more workers, in a 'pattern of practice,' knowingly hiring unauthorized aliens was committing a criminal act. Proving "a pattern of practice" would be difficult. In addition, responding to strong opposition from farmers dependent upon immigrant labor, a clause in the bill relieved employers from the responsibility of checking the authenticity of documents presented by a worker. This bill did not stem the flow of illegal immigrants.

(https://www.congress.gov/bill/99th-congress/senate-bill/01200)

In 1989 special consideration was again given to people exiting a communist country. Cubans and Vietnamese had previously been given special status. **The Lautenberg Amendment** recognized Jews seeking to exit the Soviet Union as "a persecuted group." Discrimination in the Soviet Union and the creation of Israel stirred Jewish identity. The imprisonment of Jewish activists reinforced their desire to emigrate. Emigration from the USSR, in general, was not permitted. In 1985, Michael Gorbachev became General Secretary of the Communist Party and adopted policies different from those of his predecessors. Gorbachev and Reagan brought an end to the cold war and Gorbachev allowed emigration from the Soviet Union. More than one million Russian Jews immigrated to Israel. Given the special status awarded them in 1989 (the granting of permanent residency), and the appeal of living in the U.S. led 700,000 Russian Jews to immigrate to the United States.

(https://www.rollcall.com/news/honoring_frank_lautenbergs_legacy_for_refugees_commentary-233499-1.html)

Chapter 19 – The Nineties

The **Immigration Act of 1990** also called **Reform Act of 1990** was meant to be a comprehensive upgrade of the Immigration Act of 1965. It was rooted in the belief that a high level of immigration was important to the growth of the nation. Upon signing the bill on November 29, 1990, President George W. H. Bush stated that the bill represented "a complementary blending of our tradition of favoring reunification of families with increased immigration of skilled individuals to meet our economic need."

(http://www.presidency.ucsb.edu/ws/?pid=19117)

Advanced by Senator Ted Kennedy, it raised the number of visas to be provided by consuls from 650,000 to 675,000. The cap for immigrants from each country was raised from 20,000 to 25,000 a year. Family reunification visas were increased from 260,000 to 421,000. Given the civil war in their country, Salvadorians were given a protected status. Five categories were established for "priority workers," people upon whom consuls were to look favorably in evaluating applications for immigration; they were professors, researchers, persons with advanced degrees, and highly skilled workers in fields for which shortages existed in the U.S. A cap of 10,000 was placed on unskilled workers.

An addition to the act was The Diversity Admissions Program. This program set aside 55,000 visas each year for persons who won lotteries in their respective countries. Lottery winners, who were vetted and approved for visas, would be granted permanent resident status in the U.S. Lotteries were conducted under the direction of the State Department in countries from which "too few" immigrants had recently come to the U.S. Its stated purpose was to encourage talented people from a greater variety of nations to immigrate to the United States. Lotteries were conducted in less developed nations like Albania and Algeria, but also in Poland, the Czech Republic, Denmark, Britain, Ireland, Hungary, India, Estonia and Finland. The State Department was authorized to adjust locations for lotteries depending upon immigration statistics. Between 1992 and 1994, 4,585 entered from Poland, 8,979 from Britain, 6,374 from Japan, 5,568 from Bangladesh, 6,374 from Ethiopia and 37,946 from Ireland. Because of its advocates in Congress, Northern Ireland was given the status of an independent country for the purpose of this program. The use of the term "psychotic personality" which was used to exclude suspected homosexuals was removed in this act.

(https://www.uscis.gov/greencard/diversity-visa)

To secure our borders, the **Immigration Act of 1990** added 1,000 additional agents to the Border Patrol. Under the act, undocumented persons who crossed our border were to be arrested and placed in detention. An easing in the nature of implementation was ordered by the INS (Immigration and Naturalization Service) in 1997. It allowed persons seeking asylum, who could "show credible fear of persecution and torture" in their native countries to be paroled until a scheduled hearing before an INS judge that would determine whether asylum would be granted. An INS guidance release stated that parole should be a viable option for asylum seekers who "can meet the credible fear standard, can establish identify and community ties and are not subject to any possible lapse to asylum involving violence or misconduct." This relaxed approach would vanish after the terrorist acts of September 11, 2001.

Chapter 20– Voices of Discontent

The Immigration Act of 1965 made possible the admission of millions of immigrants. The Act of 1990 made possible an even greater number in a variety of categories. While most Americans simply accepted the influx of new immigrants, there were dissenting voices

The Immigration act of 1990 called for the establishment of a Commission to Reform our Immigration System. Half of its eight-member team was chosen by the Democratic Leadership in Congress and half by the Republican leadership. In 1995 President Bill Clinton a Democrat, appointed Barbara Jordan as chairperson of the committee. Barbara Jordan was an interesting choice.

In 1966, Barbara Jordan was the first African American woman elected to the Texas Senate. She was the first woman elected to Congress from Texas and would serve in the House from 1973 until 1979. The esteem in which she was held resulted in part from her opening address in Congress in 1973. In reflecting upon the past, she declared,

I felt somehow that George Washington must have left me out by mistake. But through the process of amendment, interpretation and court decision I have finally been included in "We the people." ... My faith in the Constitution is whole; it is complete, it is total. I am not going to sit here and be an idle spectator to the diminution, the subversion, destruction of the Constitution."

Barbara Jordan gave the speech nominating Bill Clinton for the presidency of the United States at the Democratic National Convention in 1994. The Commission on Immigration which she chaired gave two reports to congress, one in 1995 and one in 1997.

(https://cis.org/Report/Remembering-Barbara-Jordan-and-Her-Immigration-Legacy)

To the surprise of many, Barbara Jordan took issue with many of the provisions of both the immigration acts of 1965 and 1990. The first report in 1995, entitled "**U.S. Immigration Policy: Restoring Credibility**" addressed issues related to legal immigration. One recommendation was for the exclusion of unskilled workers. She wrote, "The commission finds no national interest in continuing to import lesser-skilled and unskilled workers to compete in the most vulnerable parts of our labor force. Many American workers do not have adequate job prospects. We should make their task easier to find employment not harder."

(https://www.nationalreview.com/corner/barbara-jordans-immigration-legacy/)
As chairperson, she wrote:

> As a nation of immigrants committed to the rule of law, the country must set limits on who can enter and back up these limits with effective enforcement of our immigration law. Unless there is a compelling interest to do otherwise immigrants should be chosen on the basis of skills... The Commission believes admitting of nuclear family members and refugees provide such a compelling interest... Reunification of adult children and siblings of adult children solely because of their family relationship is not as compelling.
> (https://www.numbersusa.com/resource-article/barbara-jordans-vision-immigration-reform).

It is clear that the Commission Report took issue with what today is referred to as 'chain migration."

In another instance, she unashamedly stated that our society should be one "where a young black woman or man from the Fifth Ward in Houston or South Central Los Angeles...can go to public school, learn the skills that will enable her or him to prosper." 'In the absence of such opportunities, she said, the American dream was "slipping away." *(Remembering Barbara Jordan and Her Immigration Legacy, by Jerry Kramer, Center for Immigration Studies, January 17, 2106.*

(https://cis.org/Report/Remembering-Barbara-Jordan-and-Her-Immigration-Legacy)

Other recommendation suggested that total immigration be limited to 550,000 and ending the Diversity Lottery Program. The report insisted on the enforcement of immigration laws and deportation. It read,

> Deportation is crucial. Credibility in immigration policy can be summed up in one sentence: Those who should get in, get in; those who should be kept out, are kept out; and those who should not be here should be required to leave. The top priorities for detention and removal, of course, are criminal aliens. But for the system to be credible, people actually have to be deported at the end of the process.
> (https://cis.org/Report/Remembering-Barbara-Jordan-and-Her-Immigration-Legacy)

In 1966, she declared, "It is both a right and a responsibility of a democratic society to manage immigration so that it serves the national interest."

(http://usinc.org/wp-content/uploads/2014/11/U.S.-Commission-on-Immigration-Reform.pdf)

It is believed that President Clinton initially supported her recommendations, but facing opposition from lobbies such as La Raza (representing Latino immigrants) and the National Asian Pacific League (representing Asians) gave up on supporting the policies recommended by the Commission. Many of the recommendations of the Commission headed by Barbara Jordon have been given new life during the presidency of Donald Trump.

The last legislation enacted by Congress in the 1990's was the **Illegal Immigration Reform and Immigrant Responsibility Act of 1996.** This law was addressed to people illegally in the U.S. with the intent of remaining in the U.S. It stated that an immigrant unlawfully in the U.S. for 180 days but less than 365 would be required to leave the U.S. for three years unless pardoned. A person unlawfully in the U.S. more than 365 days would be denied entry for 10 years unless pardoned.

A detailed reading of the act indicates specific amendments to the Immigration Act of 1990 which focus on preventing an increase in illegal immigration. The Attorney General (head of the Justice Department) was directed to take steps designed to strengthen the mechanism for combating illegal immigration. Among the tasks assigned are training and improving the border patrol, employing new technologies including air surveillance, and training of airline personnel to detect fraudulent documents. It also directed him to share all information about his actions with Congress.

Chapter 21 – Security: A Primary Concern

There have been many times when national security was cited as the reason for a specific immigration policy. In 1798, fearing war with France and the infiltration of radicals or spies congress enacted the **Alien Enemies and Alien Friends Act**s. The first allowed the president to arrest and deport "all male citizens of an enemy nation in the event of war." The second allowed him to deport any non-citizen "plotting against the government."

A concern for national security was expressed by Justice Horace Gray in denying naturalization in the case of Fung Yue Ting. In explaining his decision, he stated that the decision of a nation to exclude foreigners was essential for maintaining its "absolute independence and security." **The Anarchist Exclusion Act** of 1903 denied admission to anarchists, persons who might endanger the lives of elected leaders and advocate the overthrow of government.

Approximately 2,300 civilians born in Germany and the Austria Hungarian Empire were detained when the U.S. entered World War I. Approximately 500 alien "radicals" were deported without "due process" by acting Attorney General Mitchell Palmer in the 1919 and 1920 before a halt was called by the Department of Labor. Advocates of the **Emergency Quota Act of 1921**, **Johnson-Reed Act in 1924** and **National Origins Act of 1929,** increasingly restrictive immigration acts, presented themselves as guardians of national security.

The **Alien Registration Act of 1940** made it illegal to advocate the overthrow of the government of the U.S. and required the registration of all aliens (usually at local post offices). After the bombing of Pearl Harbor on December 7, 1941 by Japan and the declaration of war against the U.S. by Germany and Italy, internment of enemy aliens became a national policy. Approximately 11,000 German aliens and 1,881 Italians aliens were interned.

The interment of 120,000 persons of Japanese ancestry, more than half of whom were native born citizens (without a single reported act of terrorism by any member of the Japanese American community), and the realization that it was unjust, has left an indelible memory in our nation's history.

Responding to the "Cold War," the McCarran-Walter Act in 1952 allowed the government to deport any alien or naturalized American engaged in subversive activities, and to bar the entry of persons considered subversive.

In retrospect, many policies once justified as essential national security measures are no longer perceived in that manner.

The terrorist attack upon the U.S. on September 11, 2001 made national security the single most important national issue. The perpetrators had used the U.S. immigration system to enter the U.S. legally, and it was clear that their acts could be replicated unless steps were taken to prevent them. Securing the borders of the U.S. became a central concern.

The sky was clear in New York on September 2001, and it was a near perfect morning. On that day nineteen men belonging to Al Qaeda, a radical Muslim network, headed by Osama Bin Laden, made Americans aware of their vulnerability, destroyed American complacency, and made national security a primary concern in its immigration policies.

Al Qaeda terrorists had systematically planned the destruction of the centers of political and economic power in the most powerful nation in the western world. Terrorism is defined as the creation of fear and disorientation an adversary through acts of violence. That was the intent of the terrorists. Fifteen of the terrorists were citizens of Saudi Arabia, and four came from the United Arab Emirates, Egypt and Lebanon. They were divided into four teams, each with a pilot and three "muscle men." Almost all came to the U.S. on tourist visas. Many had previously visited the U.S. To facilitate their mobility, all had acquired drivers' licenses in at least one state. Four had attended flight schools in the U.S. Had U.S. intelligence anticipated what was to occur it might have been prevented. Only one had a visa permitting study in a flight school, and the visas of many had expired.

On the morning of 9/11/2001, the terrorists gained control of four airliners and directed them to predetermined targets in their suicidal mission. One which was headed to Washington, D.C. was brought down by heroic Americans in a field in Pennsylvania. One hit the Pentagon (Defense Department) in Arlington County, Virginia, and two hit the north and south towers of the World Trade Center in New York. From a high-rise building in Brooklyn, just the other side of the East River, my wife witnessed the plane flying directly into the second building and people jumping to their deaths from upper floors of the World Trade Center. For weeks thereafter ashes floated over the boroughs and one could smell an odor released by the burning of human flesh. Two thousand nine hundred ninety-six (2,996) Americans were killed and over 6,000 were injured. It became clear that our nation was vulnerable.

On October 26, 2001, President George Bush signed the **USA Patriot Act** into law. Each letter in its title stood for an objective of the act – "Uniting and Strengthening America by Providing Appropriate Tools Required to Prevent and Obstruct Terrorism." (Public Law 107-56. (https://www.uscis.gov/ilink/docView/PUBLAW/HTML/PUBLAW/0-0-0-24178.html)

Most of the act empowered the FBI to monitor telephone communications, bank accounts and surveil potentially dangerous individuals. The Immigration and Naturalization service was given the power of "indefinite detention" of immigrants. The Patriot Act also empowered the FBI to conduct surveillance of Americans suspected of being agents of a foreign power after obtaining a warrant granted by a FISA (Foreign Intelligence Surveillance) Court. After 9/11, immigration enforcement was seen as essential to prevent terrorism.

In 2002, Congress passed the **Homeland Security Act.**
On March 1, 2003, The Department of Homeland
Security replaced and assumed the powers of the
Immigration and Naturalization Service which had been
subject to the Justice Department. The Chairman of the
Department of Homeland Security was appointed by the
president and confirmed by the Senate became a member
of the Cabinet.

(https://www.congress.gov/bill/107th-congress/house-
bill/5005)

Three agencies created within the Department of
Homeland Security focused on immigration issues in
different ways. It was intended that ICE (US Customs
Immigration Enforcement) would focus on criminal and
civil violations of immigration laws and conduct
deportations. USCIS (US Citizenship and Immigration
Service) would supervise lawful immigration procedures
and grant or deny petitions for naturalization. The CBP
(Customs and Border Patrol) would focus on preventing
drugs, weapons and undocumented aliens from entering
the U.S.

Among the responsibilities of the Department of
Homeland Security was the implementation of the

Patriot Act related to the collection and use of intelligence. Special attention was given to vetting potential immigrants in twenty-five countries in the Middle East, Asia and Southeast Asia from which terrorists were more likely to enter the U.S. These were referred to as MASSA countries. The definition of potential terrorist was broadened so as to include anyone who provided housing, transportation, funds or any kind of assistance to a terrorist. In 2004 all visitors to the U.S. were required to submit biometric data (involving fingerprints, face recognition or retina scans) which makes it easier to identify an individual.

The **Secure Communities Program** was introduced by the Department of Homeland Security in 2008. It requires local law enforcement officials to share fingerprints of persons arrested with the DHS. If a search turned up an immigrant for whom there was a hold, the arrestee would be detained until ICE personnel would come for him.

Critics of the program objected to local police becoming "immigration agents." They argued that it would sew mistrust in communities with large numbers of undocumented immigrants (estimated to be about 11 million) making them reluctant to cooperate with local police. In response to President Trump's directives to ICE to focus on deporting aliens with criminal records, California enacted laws prohibiting state and local law enforcement officials from informing federal authorities when an illegal alien would be released from custody. Many cities have declared themselves to be "sanctuary cities" in which local law enforcement authorities have been forbidden to cooperate with ICE.

Chapter 22- Barack Obama's Immigration Policies

The election of President Barack Hussein Obama in November 2008 was a dramatic moment in the history of the United States. In electing an African American as their president a majority of Americans demonstrated a willingness to turn a page on less desirable aspects of history and embrace a new and more hopeful future. Prior to taking office and conducting business for a single day our president was given the Nobel Peace Prize. Many Americans continue to remember nothing but the positives during the years of his presidency.

There were many immigration related issues requiring the president's attention. The number of undocumented immigrants in the U.S. had already approached nine million. President George W. Bush had signed the **Patriot and Homeland Security Acts** into law and had been responsible for the deportation of an estimated two million undocumented immigrants. President Obama directed ICE to focus on removing "illegal immigrants" who were convicted of crimes or were members of gangs. During the eight years of his presidency five million undocumented immigrants were deported from the United States. That number was more than all other immigrants deleted by the previous presidents combined. Until 2012 immigrant advocates denounced him as the "Deporter-in-Chief." (https://www.washingtonexaminer.com/latinos-pushing-obama-to-end-deportations/article/2600747).

At some point his thinking and his policies began to change. It may have resulted from a move by the Democratic Party away from the ideas of Barbara Jordan to courting Latino voters, or may simply have been the result of increased empathy for people fleeing poverty and violence in the Central American.

Between 2012 and 2014, 68,000 unaccompanied children were caught crossing the U.S. border. Sending unaccompanied children across a border implied a level of desperation on the part of parents who sent them. In a program coordinated by FEMA (Federal Emergency Relief Agency), children were entrusted to the Department of Health and Human Services; that agency provided transportation to locations where social service and faith based agencies were employed to care for the children. While the DHS had overall responsibility, local agencies were entrusted with locating parents or relatives in the U.S. into whose custody, after vetting, children could be released. Foster homes were provided where a relative could not be found. Children were still required to appear before an immigration judge when called upon to do so.

On June 15, 2012, President Obama issued an Executive Order creating the DACA program, those letters standing for **Deferred Action for Child Arrivals**. Under the act recipients called Dreamers, young people brought to the U.S. as children by undocumented immigrants, could request "consideration for deferred action," from the Department of Homeland Security. To be eligible, one had to be under the age of 31 as of June 15, 2015, had to have entered the U.S. while under the age of 16, had to have a high school diploma or GED certificate or had to have served honorably in the U.S. armed services. Ineligible was anyone with a criminal record.

The act granted work permits and exempted them from deportation, but did not grant them legal status of permanent residents. Registration with the UCSIS was for a period of two years. Approximately 800,000 persons qualified. Most Americans felt that the Dreamers, raised in the U.S. should remain in the U.S. The legality of the program, however, remained in question. The Constitution delegates the power to make laws governing immigration and naturalization to

Congress. Executive orders made by a president do not have the force of law and can be set aside by the next president.

States responded differently to the DACA program. California allowed its participants to acquire driver's licenses while Iowa denied them. Texas allowed DACA young people living in Texas to receive state tuition benefits for college given to all Texans but without granting them legal status.

President Obama then attempted to extend protection against deportation to the parents of children born in the U.S. who were citizens by birth. The order was called **Deferred Action for Parents of Americans**. In December 2014 Texas and 25 other states, all headed by Republican governors, sued in federal court to stop implementation of the executive order. They were granted an injunction to stop its implementation in a lower federal court. The injunction remained in effect because of the tie vote (4-4) in the U.S. Supreme Court. One justice was missing after the death of Justice Scalia, and the Republican Senate, awaiting the outcome of the approaching election would not approve President Obama's nominee to be the next Supreme Court Justice. Immigration had clearly become a political issue.

In 2008, the Department of Homeland Security created the Secure Communities Program. The program empowered ICE to obtain fingerprints from the FBI for persons detained in its custody. The ICE website states, "If these checks reveal that an individual is unlawfully present...ICE takes enforcement action" (meaning arrest and deportation.) By 2013 ICE achieved the technical ability to receive information from 3,181 jurisdictions. On November 20, 2014, ICE's ..."posture under Secure Communities was temporarily suspended by DHS policy..." In translation, it was directed not to pursue its data gathering by the Department of Homeland Security. This was a decision of the Obama administration. (It was revoked by an executive order President Trump on January 25, 2017.)

(https://www.ice.gov/secure-communities)

In addressing an International Conference on September 20, 2016, focusing on the Syrian refugee crisis, President Obama announced that the U.S. would admit 100,000 refugees. The Immigration Act of 1980 had empowered the president to make such a judgment. Three million refugees had been settled in the U.S. since the Immigration Act of 1980. In the fiscal year of 2016 the U.S. admitted 84,995 refugees and an additional 31,000 from October to January (before Donald Trump assumed the Presidency). Of those refugees, 16,370 came from the Democratic Republic of the Congo, 12,587 came from Syria, 12,347 came from Burma, 9,880 came from Iraq and 9,010 came from Somalia. 39,000 were Muslims, 46% of the total. Between 2002 and 2016, the U.S. admitted 399,677 Christians and 279,339 Muslims. (www.pewresearch.org/fact-tank/2017/01/30/key-facts-about-refugees-to-the-u-s/)

Critics accused President Obama of seeking to change the demographic make-up of the United States. Though it remained mostly unspoken, the religion of immigrants again became a factor in American thinking.

Given American security concerns in the post-9/11 era, the issue of admitting refugees from war ravaged Syria became an issue in the presidential debates of 2016. Hillary Clinton supported the president's humanitarian gestures while Donald Trump called the admission of Syrian refugees a "Trojan horse." (The ancient city of Troy was destroyed when people placed inside a gifted horse opened the gates at night and let the enemy in.)

The early years of the twenty first century will be remembered as experiencing the greatest migrations in history. U.N. sources in 2018 estimate that more than sixty million people are on the move, people seeking security and asylum (a location to which they will be admitted and protected). In the Americas, the greatest migration has been from Central American nations to the United States.

The U.S. recognizes the right to asylum as did the Ancient Egyptians, Hebrews and Greeks. Priorities for granting asylum were noted in the **Refugee Immigration Act of 1980**. The first priority was to be given to *victims of persecution, violence and torture because of race, religion or political beliefs*. This was followed by stating that consideration should be given to *people living where armed attacks and violence are prevalent* (where government is involved or is unable to control the violence of private actors), where *women are at risk,* and where there is an *urgent need for medical care.* The prevalence of violence in Central American counties was the basis of most appeals for asylum. The burden of proof falls on the applicant to demonstrate "credible fear of persecution and torture" if one is forced to return to his or her home country. Five thousand people asked for asylum, in 2009, ninety-four thousand in 2014.

(https://archive.org/stream/refugeeactof198000unit_0/refu geeactof198000unit_0_djvu.txt)

The first step in the process to legally seek asylum is for an applicant to come to an official border outpost, present a claim of 'credible fear" and to state that he or she is seeking asylum. The officer can then grant asylum or register the person for a hearing by an immigration judge. The person asking for asylum can generally remain in the U.S. until the case is decided. A judge's decision is subject to two additional reviews, after which one could appeal to the Board of Immigration Appeals (the highest immigration court). A person denied asylum thereafter could go to federal court and even appeal to the U.S. Supreme Court. In theory, all of this is possible. (https://en.wikipedia.org/wiki/Asylum_in_the_United_St ates#Refugee)

Two cases in which asylum was granted reveal the thinking of immigration judges when the cases were adjudicated. In 1996, Fauzia Kasanga, then 19 years of age from Togo was granted asylum after she made it clear that she was escaping because of her fear of female genital mutilation. In 2014, the Board, the highest immigration court, granted the appeal of a woman who had demonstrated proof of having been a victim of domestic violence in Guatemala.

(https://www.justice.gov/sites/default/files/eoir/legacy/2 014/07/25/3278.pdf)

In 1997 the Immigration and Naturalization Service (replaced by ICE, the Immigration and Customs Service after 9/11/ 2001) recommended parole for asylum seekers; it did not anticipate a flood of potential asylum seekers. People seeking admission were aware of how the system worked. During the Obama presidency most would be given dates for hearings and released in the United States. The Executive Office of Immigrant Review estimates that 22% were no shows (ICE figures were much higher). Immigrants seeking asylum were often assisted by attorneys provided by pro-immigrant organizations who advised them how to gain postponements and remain in the U.S. In a system which operated with 334 immigration judges, postponements and rescheduling created a backlog that has now (2018) reached 715,000 cases. In 2015, asylum in the U.S. was granted to 26,124. Some immigration courts are now scheduling cases six years into the future. (https://www.justice.gov/eoir)

Federal Court decisions in cases brought by attorneys of pro-immigrant organizations made the detention, prosecution and deportation of illegal immigrants more difficult. Until May 2018 few people had ever heard of the *Flores Agreement,* but that Agreement reached in the case of Flores v Reno, concluded in 1997, was the root cause of our bitter national debate in June 2018 over the separation children from their parents.

The case of Flores v Reno (Janice Reno being U.S. Attorney General under President Bill Clinton) was concluded in 1997 through an Agreement reached between the parties and approved in the Federal District Court of Central California. It began when unaccompanied minors (children under the age of 18) crossed the southern U.S. border and were arrested by the Immigration and Naturalization Service. They were detained in penal facilities that housed adults, many of whom were criminals. Pro-immigrant organizations, the Center for Human Rights and Constitutional Law, the National Center for Youth Law and the American Civil Liberties Union Foundation of Southern California filed a class action suit in the name of Jenny Lisette Flores. Representing "...unaccompanied minors taken into custody by the Immigration and Naturalization Service..." They argued for separation from adults, removal from prison facilities and for a court order requiring proper housing and care. After nine-years the *Flores Agreement* was reached with the Justice Department.

The Agreement begins with an explanation. "Whereas the parties believe the settlement to this action is in their best interests and best serves the interests of justice by avoiding a complex, lengthy and costly trial, and subsequent appeals which could last several years..." It then stipulations what the government must do to place, house and care for unaccompanied minors under the age of eighteen:

All homes and facilities operated by licensed programs, including facilities for special needs minors, shall be non-secure as required under state law...The INS shall assess minors to determine if they have special needs... Such a facility may have a secure perimeter but shall not be equipped internally with major restraining construction...facilities that are safe and sanitary...

The Flores Agreement failed to anticipate the influx of more than sixty-thousand (60,000) unaccompanied children who would be sent across the U.S. border between 2012 and 2014. It states that the term "influx of minors" into the United States will describe a circumstance where the INS has at any given time 130 minors eligible for placement in a licensed program...."

The Agreement continues, "Before a minor is released...the custodian must sign an Affidavit of Support and an agreement to (A) provide for the minor's physical, mental and financial well being and (B) ensure the minor's presence at all future proceedings before the INS and immigration court... (Case No. CV 85-4544-RJK (Px) Stipulated Settlement Agreement United States District Court Central District of California, January 7, 1997)

(https://www.aclu.org/files/pdfs/immigrants/flores_v_me ese_agreement.pdf)

The impact of this Agreement was felt when thousands of undocumented migrants crossed the Mexican border illegally and were arrested. Children remained with their parents. A Federal Judge in California in 2015 ruled that the Obama Administration had violated the *Flores Agreement* by allowing children to remain with parents detained in prisonlike facilities, and was told to conform to its terms. In addition, the judge stated that minors, even with their parents could not be housed in prisonlike facilities for more than twenty days. The Obama Administration faced a dilemma. Given that it generally took more than twenty days to prepare and adjudicate a case over an asylum claim, the government could separate children from parents, dismiss the case, or give adults freedom to travel in the U.S. with a date to return and face an immigration judge. The last two were the choices adopted by the Obama Administration. Assisted by pro-immigration attorneys, some asylum seekers were advised how they might be granted postponements. The backlog of cases to be heard by immigration judges in 2018 is 715,000.

Chapter 23 – Donald Trump: Promise and Practice

To the surprise of many Americans, Donald Trump, a Republican was elected president in November 2016. Trump was an unusual candidate. He had never held public office. He had been a Democrat who won the Republican nomination after contentious primary debates. He was a New York businessman who appealed for the votes of displaced rust belt steel workers and West Virginia coal miners. He promised to protect and create new jobs for American workers. Although he ran as a Republican, his words were those of a populist (someone who assumed the role of speaking for the "common people").

In announcing his candidacy he focused on the dark side of illegal immigration, noting criminal acts committed by illegal aliens, and pledged to stop illegal immigration. He had taken issue with Hillary Clinton over the admission of increasing numbers of immigrants from war torn Syria, and during the campaign had expressed concern primarily for the well-being of Christians in the Middle East.

During his run for the presidency, a Trump position paper was released on the subject of immigration. Included were provisions for the following:

1) building a wall along the length of the Mexican border;

2) Nationalizing the E-verify for all workers (any employer who hired a person not cleared would be subject to the law);

3) ending citizenship by birthright for children of illegal immigrants (this would require a constitutional amendment to alter the language of the 14th amendment which gave citizenship to anyone born in the U.S.);

4) ending DACA

5) mandating adult detention to facilitate deporting of illegal aliens;

6) limiting visas for foreign workers under the H1-B program (the position paper stated that such visas should be granted to people who would be paid over $100,000 a year, thereby discouraging U.S. firms from importing skilled individuals at pay lower than they would have to pay U.S. citizens.)

7) stopping "chain migration" by limiting family reunification to nuclear family members. In 2014, 645,000 green cards were issued for family reunification.

U.S. immigration would be considerably reduced if these proposals were enacted into law.

On January 27, 2017, shortly after being sworn into office President Trump issued an order suspending refugee admissions for 120 days while security procedures were being revised. Invoking the need to protect our national security, he issued an Executive Order imposing a travel ban on the admission of people from seven countries, Iran, Iraq, Libya, Somalia, Sudan, Syria and Yemen. The administration argued that those were countries in which radical Muslim organizations were entrenched, and in which internal disorders and violence made the vetting of persons seeking visas impossible. Attorney Generals in many states filed suits in Federal Courts calling upon judges to set aside the travel ban. The major argument of those opposed to the ban was that Trump's rhetoric during the campaign indicated anti-Muslim bias and the ban on admissions from predominantly Muslim countries violated the Immigration and Nationality Act of 1965.

A federal judge in Hawaii set aside the initial travel ban. A revised order, focused solely on the need for national security, made no mention of religion and included two non-Muslim nations. It also directed the Department of

Homeland Security to review the restrictions every 180 days and eliminate countries from the list where proper vetting had become possible. When this revised order was set aside, an appeal was made to the U.S. Supreme Court. The Supreme Court announced its decision on June 26, 2018, a day before its adjournment. The majority opinion in the case of *Hawaii v Trump,* written by Chief Justice John Roberts concluded that despite language used during the campaign, the language of the ban was not discriminatory and that denying the president broad discretion to restrict the entry of aliens "would be detrimental to the interests of the United States. (Iraq and Chad, both initially on the ban have been removed.)

(https://www.lawfareblog.com/argument-summary-hawaii-v-trump)

During the Trump Presidency the number of refugees to be admitted was cut from over 100,000 to approximately 50,000. Statistics from 2017-2018, the chart on the next page, indicates the decline in the number of refugee admissions.

Recent actual, projected and proposed refugee admissions

Year	Africa	%	East Asia	%	Europe and Central Asia	%	Latin America and Caribbean	%	Near East and South Asia	%	Unallocated reserve	Total
FY 2012 actual arrivals[8]	10,608	18.21	14,366	24.67	1,129	1.94	2,078	3.57	30,057	51.61	-	58,238
FY 2013 ceiling[8]	12,000		17,000		2,000		5,000		31,000		3,000	70,000
FY 2013 actual arrivals[9]	15,980	22.85	16,537	23.65	580	0.83	4,439	6.35	32,389	46.32	-	69,925
FY 2014 ceiling[9]	15,000		14,000		1,000		5,000		33,000		2,000	70,000
FY 2014 actual arrivals[10]	17,476	24.97	14,784	21.12	959	1.37	4,318	6.17	32,450	46.36	-	69,987
FY 2015 ceiling[10]	17,000		13,000		1,000		4,000		33,000		2,000	70,000
FY 2015 actual arrivals[11]	22,472	32.13	18,469	26.41	2,363	3.38	2,050	2.93	24,579	35.14	-	69,933
FY 2016 ceiling[11]	25,000		13,000		4,000		3,000		34,000		6,000	85,000
FY 2016 actual arrivals[12]	31,625	37.21	12,518	14.73	3,957	4.65	1,340	1.57	35,555	41.83	-	84,995
FY 2017 ceiling[13]	35,000		12,000		4,000		5,000		40,000		14,000	110,000
FY 2017 actual arrivals[14]	20,232	37.66	5,173	9.63	5,205	9.69	1,688	3.14	21,418	39.87	-	53,716
FY 2018 ceiling[15]	19,000		5,000		2,000		1,500		17,500		-	45,000
*FY 2018 actual arrivals[16]	6,604	42.93	2,692	17.50	2,326	15.12	560	3.64	3,201	20.81	-	15,383

* **FY 2018 actual arrivals**, as of June 15, 2018.[16]

A total of 73,293 persons were admitted to the United States as refugees during 2010. The leading countries of nationality for refugee admissions were Iraq (24.6% Burma (22.8%), Bhutan (16.9%), Somalia (16.9%), Cuba (6.6%), Iran (4.8%), DR Congo (4.3%), Eritrea (3.5%), Vietnam (1.2%) and Ethiopia (0.9%).

(https://en.wikipedia.org/wiki/Asylum_in_the_United_States)

During the campaign Donald Trump made criminal acts committed by illegal aliens a public issue. Upon taking office he directed ICE to focus on deporting illegal aliens with criminal records. He met with families of people whose children were murdered by illegal aliens to criminal gangs. In New York he met on a number occasions with law enforcement officials in Brentwood and other towns in Nassau and Suffolk Counties on Long Island where MS 13 gang members mostly of Salvadorian birth are accused of having murdered at least 25 people. More than 500 gang members, engaged mostly in drug trafficking, have been arrested.

By executive order he restored the power of ICE (as it was envisioned in the Safe Communities Policy) to pursue cooperation with local law enforcement agencies in locating illegal aliens. Many cities have refused to cooperate. In general, they fear mass deportations. They argue that if local police were seen as immigration agents, they would receive little cooperation in immigrant communities. "Sanctuary Cities" have enacted laws with one or more of the following features:

1) they deny funds to any activity that would help with the enforcement of federal immigration laws;

2) government officials are forbidden to ask the immigration status of persons with whom they interact;

3) local law enforcement officials are forbidden to inform ICE officials of the location of a felon about to be released from local incarceration.

Cities that have declared themselves "sanctuary cities" include Seattle, Portland, San Francisco, Phoenix, San Diego, Salt Lake City, Denver, Minneapolis, Chicago, Detroit, Dallas, Austin, Houston, New York City, Baltimore, Washington, D.C., and Miami. The sheer number of cities in which lawmakers have chosen to defy this federal policy makes this a serious issue.

The status of the Dreamers remains unresolved. On September 5, 2017 President Trump announced his intention to phase out the DACA program. The Department of Homeland Security was directed not to issue certificates of deferral to any applicants who had not previously registered for the program. The President called a meeting at the White House and offered to provide a path to citizenship for 1.8 million young people who had entered without legal documentation, but there were conditions. He insisted upon money to complete a wall along the Mexican border and consideration of items in his position paper on immigration. Democratic refusal to fund the wall and consider other limitations on immigration ended talk of compromise. The President gave Congress six months to act, noting that DACA would cease to exist on March 5, 2018. He said that he was throwing the ball to Congress. The date passed and Congress failed to act. A lower court ordered the continued registration of applicants and the president is abiding by the court order. Hundreds of thousands of young people remain in limbo.

The subject of DACA is divisive and painful. An interview with Daniel Garza, president of a conservative non-profit, Libre Initiative, described the Dreamers as "…innocent kids who didn't break laws." (http://www.foxnews.com/politics/2018/02/06/trumps-immigration-demands-and-whats-at-stake-in-2018.html)

The Republican Governor of Ohio, John Kasich stated that Dreamers are Americans. In May 2018 moderate Republican congressmen broke with the House leadership and pressured House Speaker Paul Ryan agree to allow a vote on two immigration bills. Each included provisions that would have given the Dreamers a pathway to citizenship. With Democrats refusing to support moderate Republic efforts, each bill fell short of the number required for passage. (The last bill was defeated on June 27, 2018)

The most difficult issue continues to be the arrival of large numbers of migrants from Central America seeking asylum in the United States. After a decline in asylum seekers immediately after the election of 2016, the numbers of asylum seekers tripled in April 2018. As indicated previously, there are two ways for undocumented immigrants to enter the U.S. The first way is reach a border post and ask for asylum. Border posts along the Mexican border are indicated on the graphic below.

At the Border

Locations of ICE detention centers and select U.S. ports of entry along Texas's border with Mexico.

Note: ICE detention centers are not the locations in which separated children are being sheltered.

Sources: Customs and Border Protection (sectors, ports of entry); Immigration and Customs Enforcement; Oak Ridge National Laboratory's LandScan population data (population density)

(https://www.wsj.com/articles/migrant-keep-crossing-southern-u-s-border-undeterred-by-risks-1529456791)

The second way, which is illegal, is to find a porous location and cross the border into the United States. During the months of March through May 2018, border arrests exceeded 50,000 migrants who entered the U.S. illegally. The media showed pictures of would be entrants climbing over existing walls. Michael Barr, spokesman for the U.S. Citizenship and Immigration services stated, "Asylum and credible fear claims have skyrocketed in recent years largely because individuals know they can exploit a broken system to enter the U.S., avoid removal, and remain in the country."
(https://www.wsj.com/articles/thousands-cross-the-u-s-border-seeking-asylum-most-wont-get-it-1529755200?mod=searchresults&page=1&pos=1)

A number of steps were taken to address this problem. Diplomatic pressure has been placed on Central American governments receiving American aid for economic development to curb the migration north. Mexico was implored to stop smugglers of immigrants and a caravan moving through its territory. The policy of "last is first and first is last" was introduced in January 2018. Border patrol officials and immigration judges were directed to address the most recent cases of asylum seekers rather than focus on reducing the backlog of cases from five years earlier.

Recognizing public interest in immigration related issues, since early May, *The Wall Street Journal* reported about illegal immigration and government policies on a daily basis. As a publication with centrist and conservative leanings, its articles credibly reflect public concerns and sentiments. Citing a number of these articles should not be interpreted as precluding the value of articles in other publications

The article (in the WSJ) *Asylum Rules Tightened for Domestic Violence Victim,* on July 12, 2018, explained how Attorney General Session was tightening rules regarding the granting of amnesty. Attorney General Jeff Sessions stated that "...domestic violence alone will no longer automatically qualify for asylum in the U.S." He overturned a 2016 Immigration Appeals Board decision that a Salvadorian woman who said she fled her country after being brutally abused by her husband should be granted asylum. The article states, "Mr. Sessions' ruling goes beyond the Salvadorian woman's case, by also overturning an initial 2014 decision by an Appeals Board that found that married women from Central America who couldn't leave their abusive marriages could apply

for asylum because they are considered members of a "particular social group."

A modification was made in deciding the status of unaccompanied juveniles. Beginning in 1990 it had been the practice of the federal government to grant "special status" and permanent residency to juveniles when state family courts recognized them as unaccompanied or emancipated at the age of 18. The U.S. Citizenship and Immigration Service will now decide whether to grant special status on an individual basis. This followed the revelation that 64 people granted resident status were picked up as part of the criminal MS13 gang.

A zero-tolerance program was announced by Attorney General Jeff Sessions. It provided that any person who crosses the border illegally would be arrested by the border patrol, charged with a misdemeanor and subject to a six-month prison term. It stated that no violator would be spared. The question faced during the Obama administration now confronted the Trump administration. What do you do with the children of parents who are arrested? The *Flores Agreement* prevented the detention of children in prisonlike facilities with their parents. A later interpretation by a federal judge in 2015 stated that under no circumstance could they remain with jailed parents for more than twenty days. Since prosecuting a case usually takes more than twenty days, the government would either have to release the accused or detain the adults but separate them from their children.

With its zero-tolerance policy the administration ordered that children be separated from parents and placed in the care of the Department of Health and Human Services. It may have been reasoned that the very announcement of this policy would be a deterrent to illegal immigrants and a factor compelling congress to act, but neither was the case. Over a period of two weeks over 2,300 children were placed under the supervision of the Department of Health and Human Services. The DHS transported children to its centers around the country from which the DHS contracted the services of private or faith based organizations. This was the practice adopted in providing for unaccompanied children during the Obama presidency. A major difference was that these children had parents from whom they were being separated. Visuals of crying babies and terrified young children being separated from their mothers produced a nationwide outcry. An editorial in the *Wall Street Journal* on June 19, 2018 was entitled *The GOP's Immigration Meltdown*. It began with the question, "Are

Republicans trying to lose their majorities in Congress in November?' It called for the administration to end its zero-tolerance policy until it could be implemented without dividing families.

(https://www.wsj.com/articles/the-gops-immigration-meltdown-1529364334?mod=searchresults&page=1&pos=1)

A solution to the flow of illegal immigrants across U.S. borders from Mexico defies a simple solution. The article, *Migrant Parents Feel Bite of Border Law (WSJ)* on June 11, 2018 begins as follows, "Texas – Norma Liticia Montoya was arrested for rafting across the Rio Grande with her sons and illegally entered the United States. A day later she was sent to Federal court here, separated from her children, 9 and 6 years old. It was unclear if she would see them again."

Kevin Appleby, Senior Director of the Center for Migration Studies (an educational and activist organization created by priests, nuns and lay people) commented, "Throwing everything and the kitchen sink at these vulnerable asylum seekers is not working as the forces driving them are much stronger than the cruel deterrence policies being deployed…."

(Appleby, Editorial, Wall Street Journal, June 19, 2018)

President Trump issued an Executive Order on June20, 2018 ending the policy of separating children from parents. Reflecting the fatigue of White House insiders, on June 25, Sara Sanders, the president's press secretary stated, "We're not changing the policy. We've simply ran out of resources."

The news article (WJS) *U.S. Suspends Family Prosecutions* on June 25, 2018 recounts how the border patrol suspended the arrests of illegal immigrants with children, and that charges were dropped against others. It notes a partial return to the policy of the Obama presidency of giving dates in the future to illegal immigrants to appear before an immigration judge with their appeal for asylum.
(https://www.wsj.com/articles/trump-calls-again-for-replacing-immigration-system-1529953925)

An article *Chaos on the Border,* on June 23, 2018 noted that although 500 children had been united with their parents, nearly 2,000 were spread around the country. Mariana, a Guatemalan woman learned that her child was in New York and was able to speak with her on the telephone. Other parents were given an 800 number to call a Center that would help them find their children. After being asked to provide information, one parent was told to "check back" in five days.

(https://www.wsj.com/articles/trump-administration-reunites-522-immigrant-children-with-adults-1529850825?mod=searchresults&page=1&pos=5)

In the (WSJ) article *Teaching Rights to Migrant Children, on July 2,* a worker for Catholic Charities described some of the efforts of her agency working with the DHS:

> "A lot of our work is on making kids feel comfortable and safe…of the total group in New York City…few children have been present in court because the court dockets are clogged. Roughly a dozen who have been to court have been reunified with a parent because they have chosen to go home to a home country. In a few instances, a child – usually a teenager- is making a separate claim for asylum and wants to stay in the United States regardless of what a parent chooses."
> (https://www.wsj.com/articles/how-to-teach-legal-rights-to-migrant-children-games-and-coloring-1530442800?mod=searchresults&page=1&pos=1)

The administration has asked the federal courts to modify the Flores Agreement, allowing children to remain with parents who are detained. On September 7, 2018, in an article in the *Wall Street Journal*, entitled "New Push on Detention at the Border," it was reported that the Department of Homeland Security is also seeking ways of conforming to the Flores Agreement while detaining entire families. One way this might be accomplished would be detaining entire families in non-prisonlike facilities until their claims for asylum are more rapidly addressed. To reduce the backlog of cases more than one hundred additional immigration judges will soon be appointed, and rumor suggests that each may be required to hear a minimum number of three cases daily.

The last paragraph in the article indicates the inconclusive nature of steps taken to address the continuing challenge of illegal immigration. It reads:

> ...the administration said ICE deported more than 191,000 immigrants between October and the end of June, a 9% increase from the same time last year. During the Trump administration's first year, 226,199 immigrants were deported, a nearly 6% decrease from the last year of the Obama administration. (Caldwell & Gurman, September 7, 2018)

There are demands from people on the political left to abolish ICE and the recent blocking of an ICE garage to prevent the movement of undocumented immigrants led to a dramatic change in the operations of the Immigration Court in New York. The article, *Immigration Court Holds Video – only Hearings* describes a new procedure adopted in New York's immigration court. It read as follows,

Manhattan Immigration court has started a new policy of holding hearings over video-conference, leaving attorneys scrambling to represent client without meeting in person. ...The suspension of in-person hearings for detained immigrants came after protesters blocked a garage used by Immigration and Customs Enforcement agents. ICE said the protests were a 'security risk." On Thursday, the first day of the new policy the waiting area...overflowed with Legal aids holding armfuls of case files...When a court official announced a hearing...legal counsel and family members of the detained immigrant would rush to the door to get more information. ...The courts have a backlog of nearly 700,000 cases. ...On Thursday, the hearings were short...detainees only had two choices in light of the video calls. They could either wait in a detention center until a future hearing or end their time in detention by proceeding with a deportation order to their native country. The intention of this Immigration Court is to expedite the hearing process and reduce the backlog. The reporting appears to have reflected what the reporter saw.
(https://www.wsj.com/articles/manhattans-immigration-court-begins-video-only-hearings1530274855?mod=searchresults&page=1&pos=1)

In the op-ed on June 27, 2018, *Are the Ends Worth the Means at the Border?* William Galson, who regularly writes for the *Walls Street Journal* wrote, "There are wrong ways of conducting a just war." This line, which is both conservative and critical deserves to be appreciated. It implies both the need for secure borders as well as a more humane and effective immigration policy. It seems unlikely that it will be easy to achieve.

(https://www.wsj.com/articles/are-the-ends-worth-the-means-at-theborder1530052771?mod=searchresults&page=1&pos=2)

Chapter 24 – An Inconclusive Conclusion

Race, religion and national security, have been major factors determining the nature of U.S. immigration laws. The immigration of Africans, involuntary though it was, shaped our history. The retreat in colonial laws from granting Africans indentures and imposing perpetual servitude shaped the thinking and behavior of Americans, both slave and free. Differentiation of human beings on the basis of race became an unfortunate reality.

U.S. immigration policies were deeply impacted by consciousness of race. The first federal immigration law in 1790 included the words "free white" as requirements for naturalization. Its interpretation in U.S. Supreme Court decisions was the basis for denying a right to naturalization to Asians (Chinese, Japanese and Indians). Only in 1943, with China as our ally against Japan, was that exclusionary provision set aside. The many laws passed by Congress to exclude Asians are evidence of the impact of race consciousness.

Racist thinking also led to the exclusion of Europeans for more than four decades (Emergency Quota Act in

1921 until the Immigration Act of 1965). This seems to have been forgotten because its sounds ludicrous that Caucasians, people mostly of northern and western European descent should have decided that Europeans of eastern and southern European descent were racially undesirable. Under the impact of the eugenics movement that is exactly what many Americans with influence and power espoused. Only after World War II and the defeat of Nazi Germany, whose ideology was based upon eugenics, did that kind of thinking lose its public credibility.

Religious persecution in their native lands was a major force in encouraging immigration to American colonies in the "new world." Religious prejudice did not disappear on American shores. The earliest of our immigration policies were developed during the colonial period. Each colony decided which immigrants should be welcomed and which should be rejected. With the exception of Rhode Island, New England's Puritan colonies were not welcoming to Quakers, Catholics or Jews. The policies of the Dutch West India Company explain the diversity of New Amsterdam (New York after 1664), while the philosophies and leadership of Roger Williams and William Penn established policies of religious toleration in Rhode Island and Pennsylvania.

"Congress shall make no law respecting the establishment of religion," were the first words in the first Amendment to the Constitution. It was decided that there would be no single established church in the U.S., thereby precluding a struggle as to which denomination would govern. It did not prevent Nativist attacks on Catholics, or intolerance towards Mormons. Religious intolerance was a factor in the immigration laws of the 1920's which were framed in a way that excluded Italian and Polish Catholics, Greek Orthodox and Jews. Opposition to the passage of the Wagner Rogers Bill, which would have permitted the admission of twenty thousand unaccompanied children from territories under the control of Nazi Germany in 1939, was at least partially rooted in anti-Semitism.

Among the factors motivating the call for limiting immigration in our own time is fear of an increased influx of Muslims. Many Americans are uneasy about Muslim immigrants and refugees, whose cultures are perceived as being very different from the Christian and liberal beliefs of most Americans. Some Americans who have struggled for women's equality are disturbed by the appearance of Muslim women, clothed in black from head to toe, with eyes alone peering through slits.

National Security has generally been invoked to protect the nation in time of war or what was believed to be a national crisis. It is a legitimate concern in our time, especially in the light of the terrorist acts of 9/11 and the Boston Marathon. The internment of Japanese, more than half of whom were U.S. citizens during World War II, is a reminder that care should be taken in adopting policies justified by national security issues.

Since the attack on the U.S. on September 11, 2001 by radical Muslim terrorists, national security has been linked closely with immigration policies. The executive order of President Trump excluding immigrants from a number of predominantly Muslim countries, recently upheld by the U.S. Supreme Court, is one example of the link between this subject and immigration.

While race, religion and national security have been important in shaping the nature of U.S. immigration policy, the economic needs of the nation have always been a major consideration. Motivated by self-interest, businessmen have most often been the most aware of the need for labor in manufacturing, farming, internal improvements and now in high tech industries. Business interests have traditionally supported more liberal immigration policies and continue to do so today. The voices of those who lobby for such policies will be heard in debates regarding future immigration policies.

Americans today are engaged in what can be described as "a culture war." Disagreement exists over a multiplicity of social issues and the extent to which government should intervene to impose solutions. Given the changing demographic patterns due to immigration, simply discussing the subject has become a trigger for emotional debate. Facts on the ground provide a comforting note. The United States has admitted more immigrants than any other nation in history, and continues to legally admit more than one million immigrants a year. One may take these facts as indicating that Americans continue to have a uniquely optimistic faith in humankind.

As opposed to a novella, this book cannot provide a satisfying conclusion. This nation's immigration policies are not frozen in time. They are part of an on-going, continually unfolding story in this diverse and dynamic society. A concluding thought! One has a right to insist that the men and women who will be making immigration policies should be well versed regarding the pros and cons of past U.S. immigration policies.

Bibliography

Books

Bankston III Carl L. & Hidalgo, Danielle Antionette, ed. *Immigration in U.S. History, Volume I.* Salem Press, Inc. Pasadena California. 2006.

Foner, Nancy. *From Ellis Island to JFK.* Yale University Press, NY, 2000.

Foner, Nancy, editor. *New Immigrants in New York.* Columbia University Press, New York, 1987.

Higgins, Jon. *Strangers in the Land.* Rutgers University Press, New Jersey, 1955.

United States Congress (1939). Hearings Before the Committee on Immigration and Naturalization House of Representatives Seventy-Sixth Congress. *Admission of German Refugee Children.* Washington, DC: United States Printing Office,

Zornberg, Ira. *Jews, Quakers and the Holocaust: The Struggle to Save the Lives of Twenty-Thousand Children.* CreateSpace, 2016.

Newspaper Articles

Seib, Gerald R. "Immigration Debate Misses Economic Reality." *Wall Street Journal.* May 22, 2018.

The Editorial Board, "Now Hiring Everywhere." *Wall Street Journal,* June 6, 2018.

Appleby, Kevin. *Editorial*, Wall Street Journal, June 19, 2018.

Caldwell, Alicia A. & Gurman, Sadie. "New Push on Detentions at the Border." Wall Street Journal, September 7, 2018

Websites

"Peter Stuyvesant – Religious Freedom". *Peter Stuyvesant*, Wikipedia, August 5, 2018, en.wikipedia.org/wiki/Peter_Stuyvesant#Religio us_freedom.

Marsh, Ben. "Colonial Immigration." *New Georgia Encyclopedia*, December 9, 2015, www.georgiaencyclopedia.org/articles/history-archaeology/colonial-immigration.

Imai, Shiho. "Naturalizaion Act of 1790." *Densho Encyclopedia*, March 19, 2013, encyclopedia.densho.org/Naturalization%20Act %20of%201790/.

Eilleen Bolger. "Naturalization Law of 1802." *Revolvy*, www.revolvy.com/page/Naturalization-Law-of-1802.

"An Act to Prohibit the Importation of Slaves into any Port or Place Within the Jurisdiction of the United States, From and After the First Day of January, in the Year of our Lord One Thousand Eight Hundred and Eight." The Avalon Project, Yale Law School, http://avalon.law.yale.edu/19th_century/sl004.as p.

"Steerage Act of 1819." Wikipedia, June 22, 2018,
    en.wikipedia.org/wiki/Steerage_Act_of_1819.

"Carriage_of_Passengers_Act_of_1855." Wikipedia,
    December 29, 2017,
    en.wikipedia.org/wiki/Carriage_of_Passengers_
    Act_of_1855

"Treaty Of Paris, 1763." Office of the Historian, Bureau
    of Public Affairs, Department of State,
    history.state.gov/milestones/1750-1775/treaty-
    of-paris.

"The Treaty of Guadalupe Hidalgo." *Educator
    Resources*, The National Archives, April 25,
    2018,
    www.archives.gov/education/lessons/guadalupe-
    hidalgo.

History of Immigration to the U.S. Wikipedia, August
    7, 2018,
    https://en.wikipedia.org/wiki/History_of_immigr
    ation_to_the_United_States

Pinterest,
    http://www.pinterest.com/pin/574349758699725
    225/?autologin=true.

"Pulitzer – In Depth." *Statue of Liberty*, National Park
    Service, February 26, 2015,
    http://www.nps.gov/stli/learn/historyculture/puli
    tzer-in-depth.htm

"Fugitive Slave Law of 1850." Ohio History Central,
    ohiohistorycentral.org/w/Fugitive_Slave_Law_o
    f_1850.

"Chinese Exclusion Act (1882)." *Immigration to the United States, 1789-1930*, Harvard University Library, ocp.hul.harvard.edu/immigration/exclusion.html

"Naturalization Act of 1870." Wikipedia, November 21, 2017, en.wikipedia.org/wiki/Naturalization_Act_of_18 70

"Chinese Exclusion Act (1882)." www.ourdocuments.gov/doc.php?flash=true&do c=47.

"Scott Act 188." Revovlvy, www.revolvy.com/topic/Scott%20Act%20(1888)&item_type=topic.

Bily, Cynthia A. "Geary Act of 1892." Anti-immigrant Movements and Policies, immigrationtounitedstates.org/514-geary-act-of-1892.html

"Exclusion Acts." Chinese Family History Group of Southern California, www.chinesefamilyhistory.org/exclusion-acts.html.

"The Chinese Exclusion Case, 130 U.S. 581 (1889)." *Justia*, The Supreme Court, supreme.justia.com/cases/federal/us/130/581/cas e.html.

"Repeal of the Chines Exclusion Act, 1943." *Milestones: 1937-1945*, Office of the Historian, United States Department of State, history.state.gov/milestones/1937-1945/chinese-exclusion-act-repeal.

"Gentleman's Agreement of 1907."
    aapcgroup11.blogspot.com/2009/12/gentlemens-
    agreement-of-1907.html

Imai, Shiho. "Ozawa v. United States." Densho
    Encyclopedia,
    encyclopedia.densho.org/Ozawa_v._United_Stat
    es/.

"Immigration Act of 1891." *Immigration Reform*,
    immigrationtounitedstates.org/585-immigration-
    act-of-1891.html.

"The Law." *Alien Contract Labor Law*, Wikipedia,
    February 6, 2017,
    en.wikipedia.org/wiki/Alien_Contract_Labor_L
    aw#The_Law.

"From Haven to Home: 350 Years of Jewish Life in
    America." The Library of Congress,
    www.loc.gov/exhibits/haventohome/haven-
    haven.html

Porter, Kimberly K. "Immigration Act of 1921." *Anti-
    Immigrant Movements and Policies*,
    Immigration to the United States.org,
    immigrationtounitedstates.org/589-immigration-
    act-of-1921.html.

"The Immigration Act of 1921 (The Johnson-Reed
    Act)." Office of the Historian, United States
    Department of State,
    history.state.gov/milestones/1921-
    1936/immigration-act.

"The Poems of Angel Island." *Don's Library*, The
    Library of America,
    sites.google.com/site/donslibrary/Home/united-
    states-fiction/the-poems-of-angel-island.

"Immigration Act of 1903." *Immigration Reform*,
    Immigration to the United States.org,
    immigrationtounitedstates.org/586-immigration-
    act-of-1903.html

"US Immigration History Statistics."
    www.emmigration.info/us-immigration-history-
    statistics.htm.

"Johann Most." July 14, 2018,
    en.wikipedia.org/wiki/Johann_Most.

Lind, John L. "Boundaries of Restriction: The
    Dillingham Commission." History review,
    Vol.6, December, 1994, www.uvm.edu/-
    hag/histreview/vol6/lund.html.

"Dillingham Commission (1907-1910)." *Immigration to
    the United States, 1789-1930*, Harvard University
    Library,
    ocp.hul.harvard.edu/immigration/dillingham.html.

"Eugenics in the United States." Wikipedia, June 2,
    2018,
    en.wikipedia.org/wiki/Eugenics_in_the_United_
    States.

"An Act to Preserve Racial Integrity." Racial Integrity
    Act of 1924,
    www2.vcdh.virginia.edu/lewisandclark/students/
    projects/monacans/Contemporary_Monacans/rac
    ial.html.

"Immigration Act of 1917." *Asian Immigrants*,
    Immigration to the United States.org,
    immigrationtounitedstates.org/588-immigration-
    act-of-1917.html.

"Emergency Quota Act – Immigration." *Immigration Laws*. immigration.laws.com/emergency-quota-act.

"The United States National Origin Bill." *Spectator Archive*, June 29, 1929, archive.spectator.co.uk/article/15th-june-1929/8/the-united-states-national-origins-bill.

"United States History." *U-S-History.com*, www.u-s-history.com/pages/h1398.html

Franklin D. Roosevelt Library. https://fdrlibrary.org/

"Alien Registration Act of 1940." *Documents of American History II*, June 28, 1940, tucnak.fsv.cuni.cz/~calda/Documents/1940s/Alien%20Registration%20Act%20of%201940.html.

"FDR Signs Executive order 9066." History.com, www.history.com/this-day-in-history/fdr-signs-executive-order-9066.

Herbert Hoover Presidential Library and Museum. https://hoover.archives.gov/research.

"Koematsu v. United States." Wikipedia, en.wikipedia.org/wiki/Korematsu_v._United_States.

"From Wrong to Right: A US Apology for Japanese Internment." *Race and Identity, Remixed*, National Public Radio, August 9, 2013, www.npr.org/sections/codeswitch/2013/08/09/210138278/japanese-internment-redress

"The Official Bracero Agreement." Farmworkers.org, April 26, 1943, farmworkers.org/bpaccord.html.

"Repeal of the Chinese Exclusion Act, 1943."
Milestones: 1937-1945, Office of the Historian,
United States Department of State,
history.state.gov/milestones/1937-1945/chinese-
exclusion-act-repeal.

"Report on the Acquiescence of FDR Government in the
Murder of the Jews (January 1944)." Jewish
Virtual Library,
http://www.jewishvirtuallibrary.org/report-on-
the-acquiescence-of-fdr-government-in-the-
murder-of-the-jews-january-1944.

"Emergency Refugee Shelter at Fort Ontario." *Safe
Haven – Penfield Library*,
www.oswego.edu/library/safe-haven.

"War Brides Act." *War Brides Act of 1945*,
warbridesof1945.weebly.com/war-brides-
act.html.

"The Truman Directive." Truman Library,
www.trumanlibrary.org/educ/dps/TrumanDirecti
ve.pdf

American Immigration Policy 1945-1950." *SHOAH
Resource Center*, Yad Vashem,
www.yadvashem.org/odot_pdf/Microsoft Word
- 3541.pdf.

"Displaced Persons Act of 1948." *Refugees and
Displace Persons*, Immigration to the United
States.org,immigrationtounitedstates.org/464-
displaced-persons-act-of-1948.html.

"Harry S. Truman: Statement by the President Upon Signing the Displaced Persons Act." The American Presidency Project, June 25, 1948, www.presidency.ucsb.edu/ws/index.php?pid=12942.

"The Immigration and Nationality Act of 1952 (The McCarran-Walter Act)." *Milestones: 1945-1952*, Office of the Historian, United States Department of State, history.state.gov/milestones/1945-1952/immigration-act

Jackson, Brooks. "Hoover, Truman & Ike: Mass Deporters?" FactCheck.org, The Annenberg Public Policy Center, July 9, 2010, www.factcheck.org/2010/07/hoover-truman-ike-mass-deporters/).

Kammer, Jerry. "The Hart-Celler Immigration Act of 1965." Center for Immigration Studies, September 30, 2015, cis.org/Report/HartCeller-Immigration-Act-1965.

"Universal Declaration of Human Rights." United Nations Human Rights, www.ohchr.org/EN/UDHR/Documents/UDHR_Translations/eng.pdf.

"Kennedy, John F. "A Nation of Immigrants." Goodreads, Inc. www.goodreads.com/work/quotes/1423547-a-nation-of-immigrants.

Ben-David, Lenny. "Lyndon Johnson – A Righteous Gentile." lyndonjohnsonandisrael.blogspot.com/.

"Public Law 89-236." U.S. Government Publishing Office, October 3, 1965, www.gpo.gov/fdsys/pkg/STATUTE-79/pdf/STATUTE-79-Pg911.pdf.

"Annual Report-on-the-impact-of-the-homeland." United States Citizenship and Immigration Services, search.uscis.gov/search?utf8=%E2%9C%93&affiliate=uscis_gov&query=Annual+Report-on-the-impact-of-the-homeland

"Chapter 1: The Nation's Immigration Laws, 1920 to Today." Pew Research Center's Hispanic Trends Project, September 28, 2015, www.pewhispanic.org/2015/09/28/chapter-1-the-nations-immigration-laws-1920-to-today/.

Zong, Jie and Batalova, Jeanne. "Asian Immigrants in the United States." Migration Information Source, January 6, 2016, www.migrationpolicy.org/article/asian-immigrants-united-states.

Zong, Jie and Batalova, Jeanne. "Caribbean Immigrants in the United States." Migration Information Source, September 14, 2016, http://www.migrationpolicy.org/article/caribbean-immigrants-united-states.

"Public Law 111-212." Congress.gov, July 29, 2010, www.congress.gov/111/plaws/publ212/PLAW-111publ212.pdf.

"About Unaccompanied Minors." *Office of Refugee Resettlement*, U.S. Department of Health & Human Services, May 14, 2018, www.acf.hhs.gov/orr/programs/urm/about.

"S.1200 - 99th Congress (1985-1986): Immigration Reform and Control Act of 1986." Congress.gov, www.congress.gov/bill/99th-congress/senate-bill/01200.

"Honoring Frank Lautenberg's Legacy for Refugees." *Roll Call*, www.rollcall.com/news/honoring_frank_lautenbergs_legacy_for_refugees_commentary-233499-1.html.

"George Bush: Statement on Signing the Immigration Act of 1990." The American Presidency Project, November 29, 1990, www.presidency.ucsb.edu/ws/?pid=19117.

"Green Card Through the Diversity Immigrant Visa Program." United Citizenship and Immigration Services, January 11, 2018, www.uscis.gov/greencard/diversity-visa.

Kammer, Jerry. "Remembering Barbara Jordan and Her Immigration Legacy." Center for Immigration Studies, January 17, 2016 cis.org/Report/Remembering-Barbara-Jordan-and-Her-Immigration-Legacy.

Krikorian, Mark. "Barbara Jordan, American Patriot." *The Corner*, National Review, January 18, 2016, www.nationalreview.com/corner/barbara-jordans-immigration-legacy/.

"Becoming an American: Immigration and Immigrant Policy." *US Commission on Immigration Reform,* USinc.org, September, 1997, usinc.org/wp-content/uploads/2014/11/U.S.-Commission-on-Immigration-Reform.pdf.

"Pub. L. 107-56 Uniting and Strengthening America by
Providing Appropriate Tools Required to
Intercept and Obstruct Terrorism (USA
PATRIOT ACT) Act of 2001." United
Citizenship and Immigration Services, October
26, 2001,
www.uscis.gov/ilink/docView/PUBLAW/HTM
L/PUBLAW/0-0-0-24178.html.

"H.R.5005 - 107th Congress (2001-2002): Homeland
Security Act of 2002." Congress.gov, October
26, 2001, www.congress.gov/bill/107th-
congress/house-bill/5005.

Duran, Nicole. "Latinos pushing Obama to end
deportations." Washington Examiner, September
1, 2016, www.washingtonexaminer.com/latinos-
pushing-obama-to-end-
deportations/article/2600747.

"Secure Communities." U.S. Immigration and Customs
Enforcement, March 20, 2018,
www.ice.gov/secure-communities.

"Key Facts About Refugess to the U.S." *Fact Tank*,
Pew Research Center, March 20, 2018,
www.pewresearch.org/fact-
tank/2017/01/30/key-facts-about-refugees-to-
the-u-s/.

"Refugee Act of 1980." Internet Archive,
archive.org/stream/refugeeactof198000unit_0/re
fugeeactof198000unit_0_djvu.txt.

"Asylum in the United States." Wikipedia,
en.wikipedia.org/wiki/Asylum_in_the_United_S
tates#Refugee.

"File A73 476 695." The United States Department of Justice, June 13, 1996, www.justice.gov/sites/default/files/eoir/legacy/2014/07/25/3278.pdf.

"Jenny Lisette Flores, et.al. v. Janet Reno, Attorney General of the U.S., et. al." ACLU, January 17, 1997, www.aclu.org/files/pdfs/immigrants/flores_v_meese_agreement.pdf.

Chong, Jane. "Hawaii v. Trump." *Hard National Security Choices*, Lawfare, May 16, 2017, www.lawfareblog.com/argument-summary-hawaii-v-trump

"Trump's immigration demands and what's at stake in 2018." Fox News, February 6, 2018, www.foxnews.com/politics/2018/02/06/trumps-immigration-demands-and-whats-at-stake-in-2018.html.

Caldwell, Alicia G. and Montes, Juan. "Migrants Keep Crossing Southern U.S. Border, Undeterred by Risks." Wall Street Journal, June 19, 2018, www.wsj.com/articles/migrant-keep-crossing-southern-u-s-border-undeterred-by-risks-1529456791.

"Racial Integrity Act of 1924." An Act to Preserve Racial Integrity, The Virginia Center for Digital History, www2.vcdh.virginia.edu/lewisandclark/students/projects/monacans/Contemporary_Monacans/racial.html.

Qureshi, Bilal. From Right to Wrong: A US Apology for Japanese Internment." *Race and Identity Remixed*, NPR, August 9, 2013, www.npr.org/sections/codeswitch/2013/08/09/2 10138278/japanese-internment-redress.

"The Official Bracero Agreement." Farmworkers.org, farmworkers.org/bpaccord.html.

Duran, Nicole. "Latinos pushing Obama to end deportations." Washington Examiner, September 1, 2016, www.washingtonexaminer.com/latinos-pushing-obama-to-end-deportations/article/2600747.

Caldwell, Alicia A. *Politics*, "Sessions Rules Immigrant Victims of Domestic Violence Can't Always Win Asylum." The Wall Street Journal, June 11, 2018, http://www.wsj.com/articles/sessions-rules-immigrant-victims-of-domestic-violence-cant-always-seek-asylum-1528754063?mod=searchresults&page=1&pos=2.

The Editorial Board. "The GOP's Immigration Meltdown." *Opinion*, The Wall Street Journal, June 18, 2018, www.wsj.com/articles/the-gops-immigration-meltdown-1529364334?mod=searchresults&page=1&pos=1.

Caldwell, Alicia A. and Ballhaus, Rebecca. "Families at Border Aren't Being Prosecuted, Official Says." *Politics*, The Wall Street Journal, June 25, 2018, www.wsj.com/articles/trump-calls-again-for-replacing-immigration-system-1529953925.

Lovett, Ian and Radnofsky, Louise. "Amid Chaos at Border, Some Immigrant Families Reunite." *U.S.*, The Wall Street Journal, June 24, 2018, www.wsj.com/articles/trump-administration-reunites-522-immigrant-children-with-adults-1529850825?mod=searchresults&page=1&pos=5.

West, Melanie Gracie and Campo-Flores, Arian. "The next Step for Separated Families:Teaching Migrant Children Their Legal Rights." *U.S.*, The Wall Street Journal, July 1, 2018, www.wsj.com/articles/how-to-teach-legal-rights-to-migrant-children-games-and-coloring-1530442800?mod=searchresults&page=1&pos=1.

Porter, Gerald Jr." Manhattan's Immigration Court Begins Video Only Hearings." *U.S.*, The Wall Street journal, June 29, 2018, www.wsj.com/articles/manhattans-immigration-court-begins-video-only-hearings-1530274855?mod=searchresults&page=1&pos=1.

Galston, William. "Are the Ends Worth the Means at the Border?" *Opinion*, The Wall Street jounal, June 29, 2018, www.wsj.com/articles/are-the-ends-worth-the-means-at-the-border-1530052771?mod=searchresults&page=1&pos=2.

"Demographics of Immigrants in the United States Illegally - Illegal Immigration." ProCo.org., immigration.procon.org/view.resource.php?resourceID=000845.

"1790 United States Census." Wikipedia,
   en.wikipedia.org/wiki/1790_United_States_Cen
   sus.

"Demographic History of the United States."
   Wikipedia,
   en.wikipedia.org/wiki/Demographic_history_of_
   the_United_States#Population_in_1790.

"John Punch (slave)." Wikipedia,
   en.wikipedia.org/wiki/John_Punch_(slave).

"Colonial Immigration Laws." *EBooks*, The Federalist
   Papers, thefederalistpapers.org/wp-Immigration-
   laws.pdf.

About the Author

Whether one lives or dies is often determined by where one is born. I was fortunate to have been born in Brooklyn, New York in December 1939, the year in which World War II began. Both of my parents were immigrants who came to the United States from eastern Europe. My dad, who was self-educated and loved history, was a worker in the garment industry. My mom, a bright and energetic woman, had been employed as a sales person in a home furnishing store, and after moving to another location, concluded her career in the workforce making what she called "overstuffed sandwiches" for students in the cafeteria of Grady Vocational High School. The fact that their son became a teacher is evidence of the opportunity afforded a child of immigrants in this nation, and the ability of that child to contribute in turn.

A graduate of Thomas Jefferson High School, I attended Brooklyn College where I received my B.A. and M.A. in American Colonial History. I was fortunate to have had an exceptionally satisfying career as a teacher and assistant principal in charge of social studies in the high schools of the City of New York. My joy in teaching history came from my belief that the facts and insights gained by my students would help them to better understand their world and make wiser choices.

In seeking to engage students in a deeper understanding of contemporary world history, I introduced an elective, "World of the Holocaust" at John Dewey High School. This led to my conducting workshops for teachers at the Eisner Institute of Holocaust Studies at the Graduate Center of the University of the City of New York. My book *Classroom Strategies for Teaching about the Holocaust*, published by the Anti-Defamation League in 1983, was meant to facilitate the inclusion of lessons related to the Holocaust in traditional high school history curriculum.

The question of whether different immigration policies could have saved more of the victims of Nazism led me to research in the archives of the Franklin D. Roosevelt Library, the Hoover

Foundation, Haverford College and the Jewish Institute for Social Research. My book, *Jews, Quakers and the* Holocaust: The Struggle to Save the *Lives of Twenty Thousand Children,* was published in 2016.

Our present day emotional debate over issues related to immigration led me to research and write *Immigration Wars.* It begins with the explanation of immigration policies adopted by individual colonies before our independence was declared, and explains the development and reasoning behind U.S. immigration laws from 1790 to present. Its purpose is to provide information that will allow the reader to reach conclusions based upon facts as to what should be the wisest immigration policies for this nation, based upon complete facts that include the history of immigration to the United States and the laws that shaped that history.